DEA Special Agent

My Life on the Front Line

Lew Rice

DORRANCE PUBLISHING CO., INC.
PITTSBURGH, PENNSYLVANI 15222

The contents of this work, including, but not limited to, the accuracy of events, people, and places depicted; opinions expressed; permission to use previously published materials included; and any advice given or actions advocated are solely the responsibility of the author, who assumes all liability for said work and indemnifies the publisher against any claims stemming from publication of the work.

ISBN: 978-0-8059-7871-1
Library of Congress Control Number: 2008924975

Printed in the United States of America

First Printing

For more information or to order additional books, please contact:
Dorrance Publishing Co., Inc.
701 Smithfield Street
Pittsburgh, Pennsylvania 15222
U.S.A.
1-800-788-7654
www.dorrancebookstore.com

This book is dedicated to my mother; dad, a proud retired Harlem detective; my family: Karen, Kawan, LaToya, Rochelle, Monique, Ayden, Kenisha, and Delon; and to all of those brave narcotic agents/officers who risk their lives putting drug dealers in the penitentiary.

The recent history of American cities is inextricably bound with the illegal drug trade that has laid waste to so many urban communities. Few have experienced the cost and dangers associated with that trade more vividly than Lew Rice, a New York native who literally put his life on the line to combat narcotics trafficking as a special agent for the U.S. Drug Enforcement Administration, which he joined shortly after its creation in 1973, then rose within its ranks to become Special Agent in Charge of its flagship division in New York.

'My Life on the Front Line' is a real-life thriller, providing rare insight into both the diligence and dangers of going undercover to ensnare often violent criminals, and where a single mis-step can be fatal. It also traces Rice's personal odyssey as an African-American man determined to help save his own community, even as he toils within a federal agency whose workings sometimes bear the marks of institutional racism.

As debate over the proper direction of America's drug policies grows ever more heated, Lew Rice provides a valuable first-person perspective to that argument. Soldiers in a war seemingly without end, he and his colleagues prevailed through old-fashioned codes of integrity, honor and courage - and by doing so, helped advance what is perhaps the least understood chapter in this nation's modern day movement for civil rights.

—Mark Rowland, Supervising Producer, BET, American Gangster

oOo

Lew Rice's well-written memoir is one of the best books to be published in some time about the history of the DEA, one of the most important but least publicized U.S. law enforcement agencies. Rice, one of the agency's first African American agents, was at ground zero when the DEA was created in the early 1970s, and using his career as a timeline, we see how the DEA has grown and developed as a law enforcement agency. Rice takes us to such important locales as Jamaica, Miami, New York City, Detroit, Washington D.C. and Philadelphia and shows the reader how the DEA operates, makes policy and faces the daunting challenges of a never ending War on Drugs. This memoir is highly recommended for criminal justice, sociology, political science and African American Studies programs and for anyone interested in reading a fascinating book about the War on Drugs and U.S. drug policy.

—Ron Chepesiuk, author of the award winning
"Gangsters of Harlem" and "Black Gangsters of Chicago."

oOo

Lew Rice masterfully captures the seedy, perilous, and volatile world of drug trafficking in this stirring memoir of his 26-year career in the DEA. The author, who began his career as an undercover operative and retired as the Special Agent In-Charge of the New York Field Office, is a gifted storyteller who takes the readers right into tension-filled "drug buys" where one wrong move by an undercover agent could lead to his or her demise.

Lewis Rice is one of the finest law enforcement officers I have met during my forty-year career in the criminal justice system; he is a creative and committed leader and a man of unimpeachable integrity. He crafts a gripping, behind-the-scenes account of the DEA and traces the history of America's strategies to combat international drug trafficking.

DEA Special Agent: My Life on the Front Line is a must-read for all criminal justice students and others who are considering careers in the drug enforcement field. Moreover, this thrilling journey into the shrouded world of drug trafficking should be read by everyone who wants to know more about the selfless, heroic, and unheralded men and women of the DEA. Lew Rice has made an eloquent and significant contribution to the criminal justice literature. Bravo!

—Dr. Thomas J. Ward
Founding Director, Graduate Program in Criminal Justice Leadership
Associate Professor of Criminal Justice Leadership
St. John's University, Queens, New York

oOo

Double dealing, corruption, murder, duplicity, ineptitude, bravery, commitment, Lewis Rice, retired Drug Enforcement executive tells it all in DEA Special Agent: My Life on the Front Line. His story is real and unvarnished. I spent 12 years as an undercover narcotics agent and played the role of the "drug dealer" and was still fascinated by his story. This book should be required reading in law enforcement academies.

—Arthur Lewis Retired Acting Deputy Administrator,
Drug Enforcement Administration, US Justice Department of Justice.

CONTENTS

Introduction

Commitment to a Cause

ON A HOT SUMMER DAY IN JUNE 1974, AT THE AGE OF TWENTY-ONE, I walked into the New York City Office of Drug Enforcement Administration and interviewed for the position of Special Agent. The senior human resource specialist, a very attractive African-American woman, led me to the interview room. She cautioned me that if I did not pass the interview today, she would not accept another application for at least a year. As a cocky young New Yorker who came of age during the Civil Rights Movement, I said to myself not to worry. If I didn't pass the interview today, I would not come back again. She also told me, if I made it through the interview, my next step would be the training academy in Washington, D.C., and if I passed that phase, I would return to New York in the best physical shape of my life. As the door opened to the interview room, she whispered if hired my main role would be undercover work and I would be dealing with "the scum of the earth." As I entered the room, I wondered, what have I gotten myself into?

On October 29, 1974, at the Manhattan headquarters for the Drug Enforcement Administration, I was sworn in as a Special Agent. The youngest Special Agent in the agency. Overflowing with pride, I felt ten feet tall. I took the train home to the housing projects in Queens, and I excitedly told my mother, "Mom, I'm a Special Agent with the Drug Enforcement Administration."

She responded with disappointment.

"Lewis, if the United States Government wanted to stop drugs from coming into the country, they could do it. You don't need to be involved in that work. It's too dangerous. Besides, you went to college. Do something else!"

Twenty-six years later, I retired as the Special Agent in Charge of the New York Division, the largest operational DEA office in the world. During that time, I conducted numerous undercover operations and held supervisory assignments in New York; Kingston; Jamaica; Miami; Washington, D.C.; Philadelphia; and Detroit. My mother's statement became my core mission: to ensure that our enforcement philosophy was formulated in the best interest of the citizens of this country.

A lot of Americans believe the war on drugs is a failure. In June 2000, I wrote an op ed piece for the *New York Post* in response to a column by Arriana Huffington, who called for legalizing drugs. I thought I laid out a clear, straightforward argument as to why a well-thought-out drug enforcement and prevention program was the only way to ensure the government's ability to minimize drug trafficking and save young lives. I was amazed by the readers' response. Ninety-five percent of the respondents chastised me and stated that the "drug war" was a failure.

Tell that to the spouses and children of the hundreds of narcotics agents/officers who were either killed or severely injured trying to stop drug dealers from poisoning the minds of our children.

This is their story.

CHAPTER 1

A New Agency Gets a New Agent

Becoming Special Agent

IN JULY 1973, THE DRUG ENFORCEMENT ADMINISTRATION WAS CREATED by then President Richard Nixon. By combining federal agencies that had responsibility for drug enforcement and drug intelligence, the Drug Enforcement Administration was formed.

I was introduced to the DEA at a criminal justice career fair at my alma mater, St. John's University. The mission sounded very exciting: working undercover against major drug dealers and building a case to put them in jail. I had also seen firsthand the danger of drugs. Several of my friends had served in Vietnam and when they returned to the States, they were no longer the fun-loving teenagers with whom I had hung out. Gone was the adolescent interest in clothes, cars, and girls. Their entire focus and daily activity was designed to purchase heroin. This preoccupation changed their daily routines. My running buddies were distracted, and I wanted revenge. After being sworn in on October 29, 1974, I spent the next two months assigned to what is known as an enforcement group, a group of usually ten to fifteen Special Agents led by the Group Supervisor. The agents would meet with informants, set up undercover operations to purchase drugs and, at the appropriate time, arrest the dealers. Since I had not yet attended Special Agent school, I could not participate in these investigations. I spent my time talking with the agents, reading reports, and transcribing tapes. Transcribing tapes was one of the most boring and tedious of assignments. The Tandberg transcriber was a cumbersome piece of equipment. It was equipped with a foot pedal to enable the listener to rewind the tape to have the conversation repeated.

All in all, those two months were very valuable and aided me in the introduction to the culture of a drug agent. This breed of DEA agents are usually highly motivated, determined, and intelligent; brave men and women who, simply stated, believe drugs are bad and drug dealers belong in the penitentiary.

The supervisor of my group was a highly decorated Army hero from the Vietnam war named Frank. His work ethic was unparalleled in the history of the DEA, and he is considered a legend in the annals of federal drug law enforcement. Frank treated me like a full-fledged Special Agent, and always encouraged me and told me that when I graduated, I had a spot in his group.

This was extremely important to my self-confidence. At twenty-two years of age, my life was moving very fast.

The DEA Basic Agent Training Program in Washington, D.C., was eight weeks. It had the reputation of being extremely tough and demanding. In fact, the instructors prided themselves on eliminating people from the program to ensure everyone that it takes a special person to become a DEA Special Agent.

On the first day of class, everyone had to stand up and introduce themselves, reveal their prior background, and state what made them join the agency. There were about twenty-eight people in my class. The class size has remained fairly small throughout the years: thirty-five to forty students. This benefits the organization in two respects: (1) It allows you to be extremely selective when determining who to select, and (2) Once selected, you can closely monitor the students during all phases of the training.

Today, although the class size has remained relatively small in comparison to other law enforcement agencies, the length of training has been expanded to seventeen weeks.

The core curriculum has remained consistent, courses in physical fitness, firearms training, federal narcotic law and the hallmark, practical exercises. This is where actual agency drug investigations—closed cases, of course—are reenacted. Agent trainees will interview sources, write reports, work undercover, perform surveillance, conduct arrests, and testify at a mock trial.

This instruction is designed to create pressure and stress on the applicant to make sure he or she has what it takes and also ensure the graduates are in the best possible shape, physically and mentally. Narcotics enforcement is a very tough and demanding job. When you think about it, in most law enforcement agencies, police officers rotate in and out of narcotics enforcement because of the inherent danger in the work and the possibility of corruption. As a single-mission agency, the challenge becomes twofold: (1) strong internal controls to discourage corruption, and (2) good supervision, to recognize when someone may be overexposed and needs to be taken off the front line.

During my eight weeks in training, we were broken up into teams and we slept in a hotel in Downtown D.C. My roommate was an experienced police veteran from the border. It was thought this veteran would impart some seasoning on this rookie.

I did pretty well at most elements of training, in spite of the fact that I had no previous law enforcement experience; however, since my father was a New York City Police Detective, I grew up hearing about crime, criminals, and criminal justice. The most difficult aspects were the physical fitness and firearms. Although I was healthy, I had never participated in an intense physical fitness program. During basic agent training, we alternated with one day physical fitness, the next day firearms. Both of these sessions were conducted by former military officers who were in tip-top shape and were on a mission to ensure that we either rose to the occasion and excelled at this phase of instruction or they would weed us out. Their motto was: "We'd rather you quit here than in the street."

One exercise that gave me and my team members trouble was called "bottoms up." Standing erect, you would squat with your hands between your legs and on the ground. You would immediately elevate yourself with hands remaining on the ground. I can still hear our instructor's southern accent: "Now it's time for bottoms up. Everybody up, down, up, down." This phrase was constantly repeated until one of us in the class could not keep up with the pace. When this happened, the class was penalized with extra exercises of bottoms up. Looking back at it now, I still grimace at the thought of those days of PT training. I used muscles I never knew I had. It was the first time in my life it pained me to walk.

The next challenge was the firing range. Contrary to public thought, most New Yorkers have never fired a gun. The majority of the class were either former police officers or military officers. Consequently, they did not need basic firearms training. After several weeks of hitting the ceiling and missing the target, I slowly developed confidence in my ability to handle the recoil of the gun, align my sights, and hit the target. This was no easy feat. I spent many a lunch hour practicing and becoming familiar with the weapon. Since this was a progressive training course, our instructors graded us and a determination was made to allow us to continue on to the next week. Mind you, the philosophy was to weed candidates out. This reinforced to the instructors that they had put together a very demanding course as evidenced by the fact that two, three, or four students couldn't keep up and had to be dropped. I can still hear that voice again: Mr. Rice, you can pass in the classroom, you can pass the field training exercises, but if you don't pass here, you cannot become a Special Agent." Just a little bit of pressure on a twenty-two-year-old. During one of those moments, when I had some doubt whether or not I would make it, I called my supervisor in New York. I explained to Frank the problems I was having on the range. With his usual steady voice, Frank told me not to worry. He said when you're in a shootout, the defendant will be so close, you could spit on him. The encouragement by Frank, a decorated Vietnam hero and respected DEA supervisor, was just what I needed. I tackled the firearms instruction with a renewed sense of confidence.

The part of the instruction where I learned the most was the Field Training Exercises (FTX). FTXs were actual drug investigations that had taken place, where the basic agents would conduct debriefings, interrogations, undercover work, surveillance, search warrants, arrests, and write detailed reports. The agency would also bring in federal judges, prosecutors, and defense attorneys, and we would testify under cross examination. To add that element of stress, the FTXs would usually start on a Friday at lunch time and continue nonstop throughout the weekend. On Sunday night, we would regroup and spend the next day critiquing what we did well and how we screwed up. Since the activities were videotaped, we could clearly see our mistakes.

I remember one scene when the agent trainees were interviewing a source with heroin track marks on his arms. The "agents" didn't realize this during their debriefing, and the instructors took this opportunity to point out the mission of DEA: "To investigate principal members of organizations involved in the manufacture, distribution, and importation of controlled substances." Since the source was an obvious junkie, he would have no credibility with a prosecutor or jury and because of his addiction, he would not be able to provide good information on major players. The bottom line: We don't work with drug addicts.

On Friday, March 14, 1975, I graduated from Basic Agent Training School #8. As I reported to work the following Monday morning, I must admit I was nervous. After playing "cops and robbers" for the last eight weeks, suddenly the games were over. I was now a Special Agent, empowered by the United States Government to arrest drug dealers, execute search warrants, and fire my weapon in the performance of my duties. At twenty-two years of age, this was an awesome responsibility and challenge.

CHAPTER 2

New York City

If You Can Make It There, You Can Make It Anywhere

American Criminal Organizations

ON MONDAY MORNING, THE FIVE AGENTS WHO RETURNED TO NEW YORK CITY from the Training Academy met in the personnel office at 555 West 57th Street. After filling out the necessary federal employee forms, I was escorted back to Enforcement Group 21. The New York office is the most challenging office in the agency. It is the largest operational office in the world, and it is where the major drug organizations are headquartered and where they conduct their business. In the early 1970s, the drug of concern was heroin.

Organized crime figures controlled the importation of heroin into the U.S. and sold their wares to African-American drug traffickers for distribution in the major cities. The daily papers chronicled their lifestyles and attendance at major sporting events—championship fights. These times paralleled the civil rights struggle and African-Americans' quest for equality.

This struggle for independence played itself out in the narcotics world also. Some of the more prolific drug leaders—Leroy "Nicky" Barnes, Frank "Pee Wee" Matthews, and Frank "Country Boy" Lucas—were attempting to cut out their Italian middlemen and go directly to the source country to arrange their own drug deals. In the early 1970s, Matthews attempted to put together an African-American leadership council, which would dominate the drug trade from importation to street distribution. However, these attempts were short lived after he became a federal drug fugitive in 1973.

My first undercover drug buy took place a few months after I graduated from Basic Agent School. My senior partner was constantly fielding anonymous calls and if possible, we would meet with the caller to determine the value of his/her information. In retrospect, this was a waste of time and very rarely yielded anything fruitful. However, we didn't have anything else going, so we met with the callers. We also conducted interviews of prisoners who would write the federal prosecutor, professing their desire to cooperate and give up the "big guy."

Usually they claimed to be able to deliver us the world if only we would get them out of jail. I was anxious and ready to begin the process of releasing the defendant. However, my senior partner, careful not to dampen my enthusiasm, suggested a better strategy was for our jailed source to work his magic from the inside. Finally, after a series of taped phone calls and meetings with very low-level drug criminals, I finally met a defendant about my age who knew someone in his neighborhood allegedly selling cocaine.

We agreed to meet in a residential area in East New York, Brooklyn. The goal was to keep the negotiations and sale of drugs on the street. However, if I felt comfortable, I could go inside the defendant's apartment. At the ripe old age of twenty-two, I felt very comfortable, so into the apartment we went. Since this was a buy-bust, once I saw the cocaine, I was to give the signal and stay out of the way as the arrest team came in to do their thing. During this undercover assignment, I was wearing a kel transmitter.

We always had two arrest signals: one audio and one visual. Unknown to me at the time, the surveillance team had observed who they suspected was the cocaine source drive into the area and enter the apartment building I had already entered.

Once inside the apartment, the two occupants talked briefly outside of my view. My original contact returned to the living room and gave me the cocaine. I appeared to examine it and began repeating the audible arrest signal. I told my contact I was going back to the car to get my money. When I opened the apartment door, I was face to face with my supervisor and his .45 automatic. For a minute, I thought I might get hurt. The arresting agents quickly moved past me and arrested the three people in the apartment. The arrest team downstairs had already arrested the driver who had brought the cocaine source to the apartment.

I was feeling great. Four people arrested and an eighth kilogram of cocaine seized. It was my case and, according to the DEA veterans, not a bad job for a rookie. On the ride back to the office, I noticed one of the senior agents didn't seem as happy and excited as the team. I finally asked him, "What's wrong?" He simply stated, "You're young and have a long career ahead of you. I don't want you to ever think this 'drug business' is easy. It's not. It's extremely dangerous and unpredictable."

The source of the cocaine, who eventually cooperated, was a fifty-five-year-old man. He wasn't in the best shape physically, and he was a previously convicted drug felon. With all this going against him, he decided to join America's team and cooperate. He became my source. In the drug business, as in life, information is power. The best sources are usually criminals who are motivated to reduce their jail time from a pending charge by setting up other drug dealers. Usually they start with their competitors, then the ones they dislike and ultimately their friends. Self-preservation is always a strong factor and usually leads the drug dealer to rationalize his metamorphosis from street criminal to a confidential source. That's one of the biggest differences basically with the "gangstas" of today and "gangsters" of twenty-five years ago. Today's generation of gangsta is raised with all the creature comforts of life and has no desire to go to jail for long periods of time. This is coupled with the federal minimum mandatory prison sentence for drug crimes, which basically ensure a long prison sentence upon conviction. The law enforcement team is successful because of the very talented and aggressive individuals they employ, and the Uniform Sentencing Guidelines guarantees that a convicted defendant will actually do 85 percent of his sentence. The only mitigating factors to reduce the sentence would be their cooperation or if they are able to prove mental incapacity.

When I started my career, the senior agents would tell the story of Herbie Sperling. Sperling was a major supplier of heroin to the Harlem drug lords in the 1960s and 1970s. On the day of his arrest, the agents also arrested his mother. With Herbie in one room and his mother in another, the agents told Herbie his mother was also being arrested and charged with violation of the federal narcotics laws. However, the agents told him they would consider dropping the charges against his mother if he would become a confidential source for the agency. Narcotic folklore has it that Herbie did not bat an eye or skip a beat. He calmly looked the agents in the face and stated, "My mom can do her time." I believe Herbie is still incarcerated in a federal penitentiary after being sentenced to life in prison without parole. Today, in the criminal world, there are very few Herbie Sperlings.

oOo

Undercover work: the process where disguises and pretexts are used to gain the confidence of criminal suspects to learn about the crimes they plan to commit. After several months of debriefing walk-in sources (a few with obvious mental problems), prisoners in jail who would promise you the stars if you could get them released, and former DEA sources whose information was extremely dated, I finally had my own case that resulted in several arrests, convictions and, most importantly, a confidential source. The supplier of the four ounces of cocaine was a seasoned drug dealer who had connections in Brooklyn and Harlem. He had previously completed a few stints in state prison for drug crimes and he had no desire whatsoever to go back to jail.

One of the frustrations of narcotics work is that unlike TV, cases very rarely begin and end smoothly and according to script. No truer words were spoken as I began my undercover work at the DEA. One of my more memorable cases did not lead to a drug arrest but gave me a very important education about the world of undercover drug work.

After a series of telephone calls between my source and an alleged drug dealer, a.k.a. S, arrangements were made for me to meet S outside the Lenox Lounge in Harlem, New York, to purchase a one-eighth kilogram of heroin. The ultimate goal was that this meeting and "drug buy" would actually result in S's arrest as soon as he handed over the heroin.

S described what he would be wearing, and we agreed to meet outside the Lenox Lounge in the afternoon. At the appointed day and time, I drove up to the Lenox Lounge in my undercover car, a 1972 yellow Cadillac. After double parking in front of the Lounge, I waited a few minutes. A man left the Lounge and walked over to the car. He asked, "Are you Lew?" and I replied yes and asked if he was S.

After our identities were confirmed, S got in the car and we began to discuss the particulars of the drug deal. S wanted me to give him the $6,000 and he would go into the Lenox Lounge and return shortly with the heroin. I resisted and told S I had the money with me, but he would have to bring the heroin to me and then I would pay him the six grand. We went back and forth for several minutes. Finally, S got out of my car and said he would go inside the Lounge, talk with his source, and see what he could do.

About forty-five minutes later, S returned, threw a revolver in my lap, and said I could hold this as collateral and I should turn over the money. I must admit, I was quite startled. I told S that although I trusted him, "my people" had given me implicit instructions not to front the money. We went back and forth over this issue for over an hour. S left my car with his gun and went back inside the Lounge. I waited for another thirty minutes, which seemed like an eternity. I was double parked in a yellow Caddy on a fairly busy block in Harlem. When S returned, he reiterated that he needed the money first and he was not going to rip me off. I maintained my position: You bring the dope, and I'll give you the money. Finally, we both agreed there would be no deal tonight. S left the car, I drove to our prearranged meeting spot, and I met with my senior partner and gave him an update on the developments.

Although we didn't have any dope, my supervisor told everyone on surveillance to remain in place and when S left the bar, they were going to arrest him for carrying a concealed weapon. The consensus of opinion was that S probably did not have a gun license. I stayed out of sight in one of the surveillance cars to positively identify S once he was in custody. A few hours later, around 9:30 P.M., S left the bar and walked to the northeast corner of 125th Street, where the surveillance team took him into custody. After he was handcuffed, I was driven to the arrest location to get a peek at him. I confirmed the identification with a nod to one of the agents on the arrest team. We didn't get the dope— or the gun, for that matter. S must have given it back to someone in the Lenox Lounge. I learned a lot of lessons from that undercover experience. During this time, the policy in my enforcement division was to submit the undercover report and surveillance report together to the Assistant Regional Director (ARD). The ARD would read both reports to get a clear picture of what was said and done during his division's undercover operations. Much to my surprise, I received back a six-page scathing note blasting me for not recognizing the danger signs. The ARD felt I had exposed myself to great danger and could have been killed. For starters, I stayed in the area much too long and increased the likelihood that the neighborhood crooks could have viewed me as an easy target of opportunity. The outward display of the revolver should have caused me to "get the hell out of there" ASAP. There is always an inherent danger in drug deals; however, when a defendant brazenly displays a weapon — watch out!

Harlem during the early seventies was a drug dealer's paradise. The combination of an outsider, double parked in a yellow Caddy with six thousand dollars on him may be too much temptation to resist. As my ARD, Ron, put it, protect Lew Rice and don't remain in any area for an extended period of time, as a target. These were important lessons for an undercover agent.

oOo

One of my next undercover cases took place in the Flatbush area of Brooklyn. My source had introduced me to a dealer named JR who allegedly could provide me with one-eighth kilogram quantities of heroin. After several meetings and telephone conversations, the deal was set. I was to go to JR's house and give him the cash, and he would make a call, then the heroin would be delivered to his house. On the day of the deal, I arrived at JR's house around noon. JR introduced me to his wife, I gave them the money, and she said she would be back shortly with the dope. As in the previous case, the surveillance team, approximately eight cars with a total of eleven agents, was positioned throughout the neighborhood. Their job was to follow the people with the money and hopefully locate the source of the heroin. My supervisor, Frank, was considered a genius in these operations and was frequently asked to lead major surveillance cases where over a hundred agents were involved in the operation.

At around three o'clock, I started to get a little nervous and wondered if I was being set up. JR had taken a few calls in another room and after three hours, I inquired, "Where's your wife?"

JR was cool and calm and said not to worry, she would be back shortly. An hour later, realizing the surveillance team was probably wondering if I was all right, I asked JR if I could use his phone to call my people and let them know there would be a delay. JR consented and I called our twenty-four-seven communications center and had a cryptic conversation with the agent in our radio room. I basically told him who I was, Lew from the 21 Club, and he should let Frank know everything's okay and I should see him shortly with the package.

A few hours later, JR took another call, told me he had just spoken with his wife, and she said the area was loaded with cops and they had been followed on the Interborough Parkway (now the Jackie Robinson Parkway) in Brooklyn while they traveled to Harlem so they turned around and tried to shake the tail. My anxiety level was in overdrive. Did JR associate me with the police surveillance? Was my cover blown? If so, would he attempt to search me or pull a gun or knife on me? Also, I had been in the house for six hours now. I was running out of things to say. I hadn't eaten and wouldn't eat if he offered something for fear of being poisoned.

I sense JR watching me to gauge my reaction, and I was certainly watching him to assess his reaction. Ron's note was flashing in my mind. I had my gun in my ankle holster. Should I pull it out now, identify myself, and take JR into custody? I decided to try to remain cool, play it by ear, and wait it out. I was also on the fourth floor, so there was no easy escape from the window.

If JR suspected me, he didn't let on. I was watching his every movement, listening closely to the tone of his voice and also closely watching his body language.

Four hours later, there was a knock on the door. I was coming down with a major headache, but I braced myself for a possible shootout as JR went to the door. I heard a voice saying, "Is Lew there?"

I now realize I had left my chair and went to the door with JR. JR must have been wondering why I was coming to the door, since I didn't live there, but at this point, I'm figuring I might have to shoot my way out of there at any second. I could sense a confused look on JR's face as he opened the door and, to my surprise, my partner, Bill, invited himself in. Right now JR should have been wondering how my "partner" knew where he lived. But I thought, as nervous as I was, things were moving very fast for JR also. Bill was about 6'2", 220 pounds, and a martial arts expert.

So it's ten o'clock. JR has two strangers sitting in his living room, both in good physical condition and both with weapons, although the latter part was unknown to him. The tables had quickly turned, and I was starting to feel better. Out of earshot of JR, Bill leaned over and said, "Frank just wanted to make sure you weren't dead." We both had big smiles on our faces.

Two hours later, at midnight, JR's wife returned and gave me the money back. She said they never went to see the heroin supplier. As soon as they realized they were being tailed, they drove all over the city: Harlem, Central Park, parts of Brooklyn. They never associated the surveillance with me. At midnight, Bill and I left, and we agreed to come back another day to complete the deal.

We got back to the office around 12:45 A.M. After going over the day's events, I took several Alka Seltzers. Needless to say, twelve hours undercover can do wonders to your system.

oOo

Lest you think all of my cases were filled with high intrigue, I'll explore the philosophy of federal narcotics law enforcement in New York during the seventies. If you think about the federal drug policy, you'll realize it's tied to violence. If the drug causes violence, shootouts, or overdoses, the media has a story to write and can humanize the issue. The politicians have their soap box, and they will create federal laws to arrest the problem, and the DEA, with limited resources, will quickly determine the leadership of these organizations, the importation and distribution routes, and implement a strategy to dismantle the entire network: U.S. based and overseas.

At some point during the seventies, we were prohibited from conducting cocaine investigations. You could not get any money for a cocaine buy, nor were you encouraged to spend resources on cocaine cases. The feeling was that heroin use caused addiction, which increased crimes. Cocaine was used by the elite, and there were few violent crimes tied to its use. Consequently, cocaine organizations became extremely sophisticated. The Cali Cartel, unlike their predecessors, the Medillin Cartel, operated as businessmen, not cocaine cowboys. They were also extremely violent but used violence more selectively.

Surveillance: The continuous watching of persons, places, or things to gain information on individuals. Frank loved surveillance. His normal office attire was a jacket and tie so when he came in with his chinos, we knew we were in for a very long night. A chino day would typically start with Frank arriving to work summoning the senior agent or back-up supervisor to his office. He would close the door and after about thirty to forty-five minutes, the door would open and Frank would simply say, "Let's go."

This meant the entire group would leave the building, get in our cars, and attempt to locate one of the people that had sold Bill or Jack drugs. Once we found this defendant—and this could take several hours—we would follow this person all day, noting who he met with, where he went, and when he went to bed for the evening: ten, eleven, or one in the morning. We would sleep in the cars and be ready to follow him the next day. These were long, arduous, stress-filled days, however, being single and twenty-four years old, I was learning my craft the old-fashioned way.

The Lower East Side of Manhattan was a dangerous place during the seventies. It was a hotbed of drug activity. My exploits, working undercover for the DEA, took me to the Lower East Side on several occasions.

During one case, my source introduced me to a Dominican drug trafficker who agreed to sell me several ounces of heroin. This was supposed to be a long-term investigation where, through surveillance, undercover negotiations, and other sensitive investigative techniques, we hoped to determine the source of the heroin and ultimately arrest him. The goal in federal narcotics investigations is to identify and lodge charges against the principals of the organization. These investigations can span anywhere from six months to two years, with arrest of the leadership as the end goal.

After a series of telephone calls, I was wired with a concealed transmitter and met the dealer inside a restaurant on the Lower East Side. Once inside the restaurant, I was ushered to a side door that led to the basement. I noticed that one employee was behind the bar and buzzed me in. As I was led down the stairs, I met the alleged source and his partner. After a brief conversation, I assured them I had the money. The "source" appeared to be about my age, clean shaven, and although he was obviously involved in a deadly business, he appeared non-threatening. Although I was maintaining my edge, in no way did I feel scared or nervous. During our negotiations on the quality of the drugs and confirming the price, he mentioned that he was going to Santo Domingo. I was trying to determine if this was for vacation or if the Dominican Republic was his home and I would not see him again. In all covert investigations, good tactics call for the designation of a danger signal. If the undercover operative is wearing a wire, the signal should be audio and since the technology sometimes renders wires useless, there should also be a back-up visual signal. In this case, I had to rely on the audio signal since even if I held up my hands and said don't shoot me, my team members could not see me.

As we continued to talk, I figured he was going to the Dominican Republic and would not return anytime soon. I made a quick decision to end the case and started repeating the danger signal. This was an extremely dangerous time. I was audibly signaling for the agents to come in with their guns drawn and rescue me. As discrete as I was trying to be, I was carefully watching the two defendants to determine if they sensed the plans had changed. As the agents entered the restaurant, I could hear voices and footsteps overhead. The source sensed something was going on, but my instincts told me he had not figured out that I was part of this new distraction. He suddenly reached into his waistband and pulled out a revolver. Instinctively, I reached over, met his hand, and grabbed the revolver. As the revolver left his hand and entered mine, I uttered the words, "You don't need that." Before he could rethink his actions, I had possession of the weapon. The agents had made it to the basement and aggressively took the two defendants into custody.

On the ride back to the office, Frank, a man of few words, shook my hand. Later that night, he wrote a two-page letter to the head of the New York office, outlining what he felt was an excellent job by a new agent. I was able to determine that the defendant was leaving the country, converted a buy operation to an arrest operation with a minimal amount of confusion, and was able to disarm an obviously dangerous drug dealer. To my surprise, the Regional Director sent the letter back with a note that read, "Put this agent in for a monetary award." (Attachment A) This young agent was off to a great start.

oOo

Another case on the Lower East Side involved me and my source attempting to put together a buy bust for several ounces of heroin. After several phone calls and preliminary meetings, we agreed to meet in the vicinity of Stanton and Ludlow streets. As the confidential source (CS) and I arrived at the building, we were met by one of the defendants who was guarding the door. He said only one could go upstairs. The arrest team, since this was a buy bust, was already in position. They had saturated the block and were also on the roof. I told the CS to wait for me as I ascended the staircase. I don't know what was going through my head. I guess since I knew danger and narcotics went together, I had no problem going upstairs to the drug dealer's apartment—alone.

Once upstairs, we exchanged greetings and he began to weigh the dope. I immediately began communicating the verbal arrest signal, hoping it was being picked up. I knew it was when again I heard the movement on the roof. I feigned surprise by the sounds, walked to the door, and opened it. I was relieved when I met my arrest team, who quickly moved past me and arrested the defendant. Although this interaction with the defendant only lasted a few minutes, I don't want to underestimate the inherent danger in undercover work. I'm on the fourth floor of a four-story walk-up meeting with a group of drug dealers with guns. Fortunately, I got out alive. During the subsequent search of the apartment, we seized about a pound of heroin, four automatic weapons, and a lot of heroin paraphernalia. This drug work is extremely dangerous business.

Because the CS for this investigation was acquired from Sterling Johnson, the Special Narcotics Prosecutor, we had agreed that his office would prosecute the defendants. The principal defendant was a year younger than me. A few months later, he was convicted after a jury trial, but the judge postponed his sentence after his mother collapsed in the courtroom. The judge stated that he was not happy with sentencing such a young defendant to fifteen years to life in prison. This was the automatic penalty for a conviction, under New York State law, for an A-1 felony. A few weeks later, I returned to see the defendant sentenced to life in prison with a minimum of fifteen years' incarceration. As I moved through my career, I've wondered at times how he adjusted to society after his release from jail.

oOo

Attachment A

OPTIONAL FORM NO. 10
JULY 1973 EDITION
GSA FPMR (41 CFR) 101-11.6

UNITED STATES GOVERNMENT

Memorandum

TO : Lewis Rice
Special Agent

DATE: March 24, 1976

FROM : Francis E. White
Group Supervisor

SUBJECT: Letter of Commendation - Special Agent Lewis Rice

At this time I would like to commend you for the judgment, courage and decisiveness you displayed during the arrest of [redacted] on March 23, 1976 in C1-[redacted]

During March, 1976 you developed SC1-[redacted] as a cooperating individual and as a result of your direction the Informant initiated this investigation. Subsequent to completing the appropriate background investigation, on the evening of March 23, the Informant introduced you to [redacted] and [redacted] for the purpose of purchasing two ounces of heroin. During your undercover negotiations with [redacted] you were able to ascertain that the principal defendant, [redacted] was preparing to leave the United States shortly for the Dominican Republic. You displayed professional acumen and judgment in immediately communicating this information and at the same time recommending that the case be terminated to preclude [redacted] from becoming a possible fugitive. In addition, your judgment was excellent in conserving our limited resources utilized for the purchase of evidence.

You conformed with our Standing Operating Procedures established within the Group and the arrest plan formulated while you were in an undercover capacity was implemented without confusion in a minimum of time.

After being displayed two ounces of heroin in the basement of [redacted] [redacted] in the Lower Eastside section of Manhattan you transmitted the arrest signal and as the arresting agents descended the stairs into the basement you observed [redacted] draw a revolver from the waist band of his trousers and turn to confront the agents who were about to enter the back room of the basement. Your courage and quick reaction in grabbing the revolver from [redacted] hand thwarted a volatile situation and may have saved the life of one of your fellow Group members.

I again commend you for your courage in disarming [redacted] for although you most certainly experienced the fear of danger you were able to proceed

Attachment A

in the face of it with calmness and decisiveness and were able to act properly in this threatening situation.

A copy of this memorandum will be placed in your personnel file.

cc: 01
cc: 02
cc: 03
cc: 04
cc: 20
cc: 94
cc: Special Agents
Group 23

In the 1970s, a group of senior African-American agents filed a lawsuit in the District Court in Washington, D.C., against the DEA. The African-American agents alleged that the agency had discriminated in hiring, training, promotions, discipline, awards, and assignments. The culture of the agency when I started was that undercover work was not respected by the agency for advancement. It was common knowledge that some officials had expressed their belief that "a monkey could buy drugs." What lunacy. Undercover work is still the most dangerous assignment in narcotics work. If an agent is going to be killed or wounded, it will most likely come from undercover narcotics work. Yet those who put their lives on the line conducting themselves as undercover operatives found it extremely difficult, if not impossible, to get promoted. Consequently, there was a lot of turmoil and dissention in the DEA regarding racial issues.

When the trial was over, the agency was found guilty, ordered to develop and implement non-discriminatory human resource policies, immediately promote numerous African-American agents who were held back, and pay them for years of discrimination and poor treatment. The agency's response to the court's findings has also been a source of debate and, depending on the leadership of the agency, a cause for sinking morale problems in the workforce since it has not complied with the spirit of the court order. From 1982 to the present, the District Court in Washington, D.C., has held oversight of the agency, and a committee of African-American Special Agents meets every quarter to ensure agency compliance with the court order.

Enlightened leadership has learned that sound human resource policies create good morale amongst employees. This good morale empowers the agents to do their jobs with zest, and this energetic spirit benefits our citizens. Bottom line: It's a win-win situation when you treat people fairly.

One of my cases resulted in a confidential source (CS) who kept me busy for two years conducting undercover investigations and testifying at trials. After a few successful undercover assignments under my belt, my senior partner, Bill, took me under his wing and said the key is to be the case agent, not the undercover agent. If you could do both, that was okay, but you had to control the case. This way you would receive full credit for the successful development of the investigation. This was one of those pearls of wisdom that would guide me as I pursued my many drug investigations.

Since the source was acquired from one of my cases—all of the cases he conducted were mine. With this source, I hit pay dirt. He had an eight-page FBI rap sheet and had been arrested by the Federal Bureau of Narcotics for marijuana distribution in the fifties. He had a strong reputation and track record in the criminal drug world. He was also an educator for me in the way of the drug culture and the street.

Because of his age and prior problems with the criminal justice system, he quickly made the decision to cooperate. The idea of spending several years in a federal prison was enough for him to quickly assess the situation and "join America's team."

I spent the next year making drug buys throughout East Harlem and Brooklyn, purchasing multi-ounce quantities of heroin. Each drug buy was reinforced with a second buy—two sales to a federal agent. The choice would be clear: either cooperate or get ready for a fifteen-year prison sentence in the federal pen.

My CS's reputation was so solid in the drug world that every drug buy went like clockwork. The experienced senior agents could not believe it. They realized I had a goldmine. As the rap sheets of these defendants began to come in, I was amazed that the overwhelming majority of these criminals had been previously arrested by either the Bureau of Narcotics and Dangerous Drugs or the Federal Bureau of Narcotics, both predecessors of the DEA. These were not the guys standing on the corner selling their wares. These were the mid-level dealers whom you would conduct a drug transaction—by appointment only.

Fifteen months into the investigation, after numerous buys throughout East Harlem, we arranged to arrest sixteen defendants. The arrests went like clockwork. Either I would arrange a meeting and the arrest team would lock the defendant up or the team would descend on his house or his neighborhood hang out and then bring them in.

One by one, they were brought to the office at 57th Street, fingerprinted, photographed, and then brought to the U.S. Courthouse, Southern District of New York for arraignment. I stood with the Assistant United States Attorney as the charges were read, beaming with pride. However, my pride slowly dissipated as each defendant was released after signing a surety bond—no collateral was posted.

The last one of the group to be released had been arrested twice before for violation of the federal narcotics law. In fact, he was presently on federal parole; in the same building where the arraignment was being conducted. He had a rap sheet indicating an arrest record going back thirty years.

I had been taught that a good defense attorney's job is to turn shit into sugar. I got a first-hand look at one of the best. The defense attorney, used the defendant's thirty-year involvement in the criminal justice system and his parole status as a badge of honor. He emphatically stated that nowhere on this rap sheet was there a notice that his client was a fugitive and had failed to show up to court. He continued that he had spoken to his parole officer and the parole officer had stated that his client had never missed a scheduled visit. He concluded by saying his client was a "champion" when it came to reporting to court.

With that, the magistrate released his client. I could not believe my eyes. I had spent over a year of my life purchasing large quantities of drugs throughout the city from some very dangerous characters, and the magistrate released all of them on their signature. He must have read the astonished and perplexed look on my face because he invited me back to his chambers. He told me he personally wanted me to know the citizens of the United States appreciated the work I had done on their behalf, but he was working under some very strict guidelines. Since the defendants had roots in the community, he was forced to release them pending trial.

As the cases proceeded through the criminal justice system, the "champion" became a fugitive. I ran into his attorney during my rounds at the Southern District of New York, and I asked him what happened to the "champion." He gave me a polite smile, shrugged his shoulders, and descended the courthouse steps.

One of my favorite parts of the criminal justice process was the trial. Since the "case agent" was familiar with all aspects of the investigation, he/she also had the responsibility of implementing the strategy and the successful development of the case. Once the arrests were over, a considerable amount of time was spent debriefing the arrested defendants and attempting to elicit their cooperation. Defendants who agreed to cooperate and testify had to be prepared in the art of testimony. I say art because the trial is theater. Close attention is paid to your apparel and your courtroom demeanor. You must also ensure that witnesses are familiar with their testimony and anticipate the defense attorney's questions and your witnesses' responses. Since most accomplice witnesses have never testified, this could be quite a challenge. Unprepared witnesses can submarine an otherwise airtight case.

The case agent is allowed, in federal court, to sit at the prosecution table during the trial. Although the agent cannot question the witnesses, he plays a pivotal role in the presentation of the government's case. There is an overwhelming sense of satisfaction, sitting at the prosecution table, watching the witnesses testify, suggesting trial strategy with the prosecutor, and seeing the case unfold before the judge and jury.

The voir dire is when the lawyers get to question the prospective jurors prior to their selection to serve on the jury. During one case, it appeared to me the prosecutor was arbitrarily excluding African-Americans. Several of the defendants were African-American men. Could it be the prosecutor believed an African-American juror would automatically identify and have sympathy for the defendants solely because of race?

My experience has been that African-Americans take their responsibility as jurors very seriously. They listen intently to the testimony and the judge's instructions. If they believe the case was investigated fairly, they will decide guilt or innocence based on the evidence. However, if the prosecution basically "winks at the jury" and says, by its presentation of the case, basically "go with us on this guys. We know they're guilty," they will and should acquit in a second.

After I explained my concerns to the prosecutor, the jury was empanelled with several African-Americans. Although I was convinced of the defendant's guilt, I believed the jury felt the presentation of the evidence was straightforward and there was not any overreaching on the part of the government. Although I never had any communication with the jury, I do believe my presence and testimony aided their sense of fair play.

oOo

The New York Division of the DEA is the largest office in the world. The pressures from headquarters on investigations and the relationship with other law enforcement agencies, most notably the New York City Police Department and the Federal Bureau of Investigation are, always front and center.

Although the DEA was a relatively young agency, the mission required the agents to be very proactive, to push the envelope in order to be successful. The mentality sometimes rubbed off in the relationships with other law enforcement officers and the police department. The attitude sometimes was not one of cooperation but of dominance. We were constantly at "war" and the more we fought, sometimes the more the bosses enjoyed it.

During the late seventies, the racial tensions in the office, was at times, overwhelming. Agents who would eagerly work undercover in some of the toughest neighborhoods in the city hesitated to have discussions in the hallways, lest they be seen by management talking to another agent who was viewed as on the "enemy's" team. If you wanted to talk with someone about a sensitive issue, you either agreed to meet at the store outside the office or in the office gym. Can you imagine the stress? You're under stress working undercover, where a mistake could get you killed, and you're under stress in the office if you're observed by a boss having a conversation with the "enemy," another agent deemed to be on the "B" team.

The Special Agent in charge was white and the second in command was black. Both were over six feet tall and quick to express their opinion and operate with the power of their strong personalities and beliefs. They were at war — the office was divided. Consequently, in spite of our successes, there was no way we were operating at peak efficiency. I wanted out. I enjoyed what I was doing, but needed a break. Unrelated to these issues, my division was scheduled to be reorganized. This happens every so often, not related to corruption but usually as a response to a new drug threat or a special enforcement program initiated by Washington.

My second line supervisor, who became one of my mentors, asked me where I would like to go. In addition to the three enforcement groups in the city, he also had responsibility for the Long Island District office and the Conspiracy Group, located at the Federal Courthouse in the Eastern District of New York (Brooklyn). This was an easy decision for me. I suggested the conspiracy group.

I had spent the last four years on the front lines. A shirt-and-tie group at the courthouse sounded very appealing. Besides, Brooklyn is my favorite borough. I think he was a little surprised, and he suggested I might want to consider going to the Long Island office. He told me another black agent had recently transferred there and could use some help working undercover.

I thought about it and considered the Conspiracy Group as a better career move. I also found out there had never been a black agent assigned to this shirt-and-tie group and that the supervisor, Fred, was African-American. Fred ensured that I received recognition for my cases and is one of the few people from the "old days" with whom I am still in contact. It took a few months, but I did receive a transfer to the Eastern District Conspiracy Unit (EDCU). The office was located in the basement of the courthouse with no windows. We shared the space with the court interpreters and a side door emptied out to the U.S. Marshal's office. There were a half-dozen senior agents in the group, and they welcomed me with open arms. I felt like a senior agent also. We worked closely with the federal prosecutors in the narcotics division, debriefing convicted defendants who claimed they wanted to cooperate and give up the "main man." We would also generate our own cases from confidential sources. The advantage was we were encouraged to travel, interview witnesses, and develop cases without the normal push for arrest numbers. We were also a valuable resource for the prosecutors and were constantly called on to train the new Assistant United States Attorneys assigned to the drug unit.

The group had had a lot of success and was respected by the senior prosecutors and federal judges. This was shaping up to be a great assignment. I had told myself that with this transfer, I would no longer work undercover but solely operate as the case agent. For the most part, I was able to fulfill that promise, absent a few buy-bust cases, which were very short undercover roles. I structured my assignment to long-term cases, where we would lodge federal charges against the principals—the mission of the DEA.

Hyman Liberman v. U.S. of America

One of the long-term cases I developed involved a group of Harlem drug dealers the New York City Police Department's Narcotics Unit had spent the year recording and observing their receipt of mannite and quinine. Although mannite and quinine were the essential dilutants used to "cut" heroin, there was no state law against the possession and sale of these substances. The city detectives, well aware of the narcotic backgrounds of the recipients, brought the case to the conspiracy unit to explore the possibility of federal charges. Conspiracy cases allow the testimony of witnesses to substantiate the government's allegation of criminal wrongdoing. Very few prosecutors, however, are comfortable lodging drug charges against defendants when no drugs or money have been seized. Juries, especially New York juries, like to see the fruits of drug crimes. The visual display of drugs or money in a courtroom lends credence to the government's case.

This case would rely strictly on the testimony of criminal witnesses, police officers, and agents. Missing would be those typical spoils of the drug trade: money, drugs, and guns. After discussing the strengths and weaknesses of the case with the chief of the narcotics unit for the Eastern District of New York, the office agreed to prosecute the case and assigned a veteran prosecutor to lead the government effort.

The theory of the prosecution was based on four essential elements: (1) the reputation of the defendants in the criminal drug world, (2) the legitimate commercial value for mannite and quinine and the price the defendants were paying, (3) the large amount of these dilutants that were purchased by the defendants, and (4) mannite and quinine are used to cut heroin.

The police department also provided a witness who had spent the year making these deliveries throughout the city. In an attempt to enhance their case against the defendants, they directed the witness to ask," What are you doing with this stuff?" and to engage these men in discussion to learn about their drug business. On each attempt, the dealers refused to discuss their activities. They either gave the witness the silent treatment or mumbled a few insignificant words. We had photographs of the meetings with the witness, and police surveillance reports documenting the deliveries, but we were missing a live witness who could connect them to the drug trade.

I spent several weeks researching old DEA case files and talking to narcotic prosecutors in the Eastern and Southern Districts who had specialized in Harlem drug cases. One name kept coming up: Frank. He was being held in protective custody in a federal jail on the West Coast. And in his heyday, he was considered one of the nation's most prolific drug dealers.

Although he had been incarcerated for several years, having been sentenced to forty years in the Southern District of New York and thirty years by the state of New Jersey, he had a good handle on what was going on in the street and was, more importantly, able to provide that crucial link to the defendant's dealings in the drug world. Through direct testimony, he was able to provide valuable insight into the heroin distribution operation and the role and reputation of the defendants. We hit pay dirt. After several months of preparing the witnesses for testimony at trial, searching for documentary evidence that would substantiate that a defendant was in a particular place at a certain time, and analyzing the police reports, the case was indicted by a grand jury and eight defendants were charged with possession of narcotics (heroin) with the intent to distribute. This marked the first time individuals were indicted on federal drug charges solely for their dealings in mannite and quinine. We were traveling in uncharted waters; however, with an aggressive and experienced prosecutor, we knew we were moving in the right direction.

As the case agent, I was responsible for assisting the government prosecutor in assembling the prosecution's case. Another central witness was an old-time conman who loved to talk. Because of the violent nature of drug dealers and their reach, we had relocated this witness to another state. Five days a week, I would meet him at the parking lot of the Holiday Inn near LaGuardia Airport and take him to the federal courthouse, where we would spend the day preparing for trial.

During trial preparation, the prosecutor and the case agents usually develop a tight bond. Every aspect of the case is discussed, and all the evidence is painstakingly reviewed to determine relevancy and impact on the jury. The witnesses must also be thoroughly prepared—you must know what they are going to say and how well they are going to say it. The bottom line is no surprises. It's customary for accomplice witnesses to minimize their involvement in criminal behavior. The key job of the prosecutor, however, is to have their witness disclose the full extent of their criminal activity during the government's phase of the trial and to accurately predict the questions the defense will ask.

This was a challenge. Although we had police surveillance photographs to back up the witness' testimony, his penchant for being extremely talkative could spell trouble. A key part of our meetings was to get him to limit his answers to the questions posed and not volunteer information. Changing a lifetime behavior is never easy.

The day of the arrest, we assembled a team of DEA agents and New York City detectives who were spread throughout the city, attempting to locate and arrest these dealers for purchasing large amounts of mannite and quinine several years earlier. To say the least, they were quite astonished after being arrested for purchasing mannite and quinine. I had assembled a team to arrest the lead defendant and had previously taken pictures of his estate in Englewood Cliffs during a helicopter surveillance. I still remember the helicopter pilot asking me as we entered the chopper at the 61st Street heliport in the city, "Do you know how to get there?"

I smiled and answered, "Not by helicopter." Much to my surprise, we traveled the same route as if we were traveling by car—up the George Washington Bridge and then onto Route 4.

As to be expected, our lead defendant was living large. Conducting his heroin business in Harlem, he would retreat to this exclusive neighborhood mansion with a tennis court and several luxury vehicles, including a Rolls Royce. Not a bad life for a heroin dealer in 1978.

On the day of the arrest, the Englewood PD joined us as we arrested him at his house, seized his Rolls, and executed a search warrant throughout his property. During the search, one of the starters for the New York Knicks arrived to play tennis. He had no involvement in the drug business, but he had the unfortunate luck of arriving to play tennis on the same day the Feds were busy at work.

True to form, as with most drug dealers who are at the top of their game, our lead defendant had nothing to say beyond providing biographical information. Since he knew the case was about the dealings in mannite and quinine, I'm sure he thought as soon as his lawyer arrived, he would be released and this case would just fade away into the sunset. Mannite and quinine—not a big deal.

All of the defendants pled not guilty so four months later, we headed for trial. The trial lasted about three and a half weeks and resulted in the conviction of seven defendants and the acquittal of one.

The government's case was powerful but straightforward. Our lead witness, a former heroin kingpin who dominated the Harlem drug world, detailed the inner workings of the organization, how the business was conducted, and who the key players were and their top lieutenants. The courtroom, including the judge, was fascinated by this testimony. There was testimony about a well-known defense attorney who was involved in the heroin business. The judge, who had seen this attorney practice in his courtroom on many occasions, was so surprised he questioned the witness to make sure what he had heard. Drugs yield enormous amounts of money, and money will make the blind see. It's an old familiar story, one that gets replayed every day.

It's always been amazing to me when defendants take the witness stand and explain their version of the events. This case was no exception. One of the defendants tried to mitigate the charges by claiming his post-arrest statements were made without being advised of his Constitutional rights. The prosecutor then went through the arrest step by step.

"Now, Mr. X, did you hear the words, 'You have the right to remain silent'?"

Mr. X stated, "Yes."

The prosecutor continued. "Now when you heard these statements, who was in the car with you?"

Mr. X stated there was a police officer driving the car and there was a police officer in the back seat with him.

"So, Mr. X, who did you think he was talking to, the other police officer?"

The courtroom erupted in laughter. Even the judge put a smile on his face.

My experience has been that the dealers of the major drug organizations are extremely intelligent and good managers. If they had channeled that energy into legitimate efforts, they would have probably been CEOs of major corporations. I arrested one of the defendants walking down a street in midtown Manhattan reading the *Wall Street Journal.* On sentencing day, the defendants received prison terms and fines which ranged from five to fifteen years and $25,000 in fines.

oOo

Another case began with my source, who was able to infiltrate a drug organization. His contact was an Hispanic dealer, so we selected a Hispanic agent. This was set up as a buy-bust in Jackson Heights, Queens. As usual, my source had done his homework, and the case went like clockwork. The undercover agent met the defendant at the appropriate time, and the surveillance agents noticed an individual parked in the immediate area. Sensing he might be part of the deal, they had one of the surveillance agents keep an eye on him. Narcotic agents develop that keen sense of observation and intuition. They become psychology experts and masters of the art of nonverbal communication. A man was sitting in a car in the driver's seat, a very common occurrence in the city. However, when drugs are involved, there may be a connection. That intuition paid off.

When the heroin was exchanged and the arrest signal was given, the man quickly started the car and pulled off. Still not realizing the exact connection but believing something was amiss, we arrested the driver and brought him to our office in Brooklyn. As we began an inventory of his personal contents, he grabbed his telephone book and attempted to scratch out a number. We were now becoming sure he was involved in the deal. Both defendants were lodged that night and charged with federal possession with intent to distribute a pound of heroin.

In preparation for trial, we sent the telephone book to the FBI laboratory in Quantico. We were attempting to determine what numbers the defendant tried to cross out. We hit pay dirt. The FBI laboratory was able to restore the numbers. This was the telephone number for the other defendant. Armed with this evidence, we proceeded to trial. The testimony lasted a few days, and the jury came back with guilty verdicts against both defendants. The man in the car was also a known associate of Johnny Gramatikos, a major Greek heroin trafficker who was a major supplier of large quantities of heroin to organized crime.

The defendants were sentenced to prison terms of eight and twelve years. After a few weeks in prison, the principal defendant expressed his desire to join "America's team." Evidently twelve years in prison was not too appealing. He was willing to cut his losses and tell all he knew.

We took him out of the federal jail in New York and relocated him to a federally approved facility in another state. For the next six months, I made a weekly trip to take him out of jail and to the local DEA office, where I would debrief him as to his involvement in the drug trade.

As the case agent, I would also travel to places like Richmond, Virginia, where the heroin entered the U.S. on a ship that arrived at the Port of Richmond. In Richmond, we were able to locate a witness who lent our witness his car while he was in Richmond. We were also able to obtain the hotel and telephone records that corroborated their travel in Richmond and contact with other defendants.

After eight months of investigation, we indicted a dozen organized crime figures for possession with intent to distribute twelve kilograms of heroin.

The heart of our case was the accomplice witness who spent several days on the witness stand with each defense attorney, trying to poke holes in his story.

Our witness blew up on a couple of occasions. The defendants would taunt him with hand motions, simulating cutting someone's tongue, and one of the defense attorneys referred to him as the weasel. In spite of all this drama, the jury was able to follow the evidence and come back with guilty verdicts against each defendant.

oOo

It was 1982. After being denied a promotion earlier, the DEA conducted an agency-wide review that resulted in seven agents being immediately promoted. In the span of thirty days, I was promoted and received a sought-after transfer to Kingston, Jamaica. I was ready to leave the streets of New York for the warmth of the Caribbean. But my transfer was delayed for a couple of months because of a very dangerous incident that occurred off-duty.

In June 1982, after leaving a transfer celebration in Brooklyn near Dekalb Avenue, I was approached by a group of five men in an apparent robbery. They formed a semicircle around me and the one who had his hand in his jacket, pointed at me, said "This is it." Although I had my gun on me, I didn't want to draw it right away. My plan was to cooperate, give them my money and, at the appropriate time, pull my gun and make the arrests. I gave them my money, watch, and ring. I had an open-neck shirt, and one of them noticed I was wearing a chain. My mother had given it to me, and I was very attached to it. He yanked it off my neck. As they became more aggressive, they patted my waist and felt my gun, simultaneously, I stepped back as he yelled, "He's got a gun!" Suddenly, I tripped and fell backward with the defendant on top of me. As we were wrestling to get possession of the gun, I saw the others run away, but one of them made a u-turn and headed back in my direction. I didn't want him to return and either shoot me or stab me while his partner was on top of me, so I increased my efforts to get control of the gun and start firing. I hit my assailant three times, once in the chest, which killed him. In the struggle, somehow I also managed to get shot in the thigh, though luckily I didn't hit any bone, so it wasn't that serious.

The others had all run out of sight. I knew there was a police station nearby, and I commandeered a car, which was not so hard to do when you had a gun drawn and you were yelling, "Police, police." We drove to the station and I ran in, bleeding, with my pants all torn up, shouting loudly that I was an agent with the DEA who had just shot a man who had robbed me. I wanted to go after the others, but the police were more of a mind to take my gun and call an ambulance to take me to the hospital.

My plan had been to let them take my belongings and then, when they were running away, take out my gun and go after them, figuring I could catch the slowest one and he would eventually lead me to the rest of the pack. But when they searched me, that had put an end to that plan. And as I said, the entire incident, which seemed like a lifetime but probably only lasted a minute or two, delayed my reassignment to Jamaica. I needed several months to fully recover from the wound.

In twenty-six years with the DEA, that was the only time I ever shot anyone, and ironically it was a mugger instead of drug dealer. I was ready to leave the streets of New York City.

CHAPTER 3

International Operations

Politics and Drugs: A Losing Combination

ALL OVERSEAS ASSIGNMENTS ARE COMPETITIVE SELECTIONS WHERE THE JOB is advertised and agents apply to the Human Resources office in Washington. For non-supervisory positions, selections are made by the Chief of Operations after consultation with the Country Attaché in the foreign office.

Garfield, the Country Attaché in Kingston, Jamaica, had traveled back to New York to testify at a narcotics trial in the Southern District of New York. He was one of those legendary narcotics agents who had distinguished himself as a prolific undercover and case agent in the New York office. I ran into him and casually mentioned that I had put in for the job in his office. Garfield was non-committal but reassuring. A month later, things were really looking up. After eight years of conducting numerous dangerous undercover assignments and being denied a promotion, I was promoted and transferred to sunny Jamaica in the span of a month.

The Mansfield Amendment sets the terms for the conduct of American agents overseas. Simply said, American agents are forbidden to conduct investigations without the consent of the host government.

Unlike investigative operations in the United States, where notifications of local government leaders are not required, in foreign countries all investigative steps must be approved by government authorities.

The DEA office was located inside the Mutual Life Insurance Building at Oxford Road in Kingston, Jamaica. This was the home of the U.S. Embassy.

The Island of Jamaica is home to approximately 1.5 million people. The mainstay of the economy is tourism, so the officials are extremely concerned about the country's image as it relates to drugs and crime. In 1982, the country had recently concluded an election where hundreds of people were killed.

The Jamaica Labor Party, headed by Prime Minister Edward Seaga, was in power. Since Seaga was considered pro-American, the U.S. Government did not push him on the drug issue. Our strategy was to facilitate investigations developed in the U.S. and solicit the cooperation of the Jamaica Constabulary Force (JCF) and the military: Jamaica Defense Force (JDF).

To accurately portray the JCF's Narcotics Unit, it was composed of approximately twenty-nine officers based in Kingston with six cars. What they lacked in resources the Jamaican Police made up in heart. This is the only police department in the world where the officers patrol with M-16 machine guns. No matter what the assignment, the JCF were always ready to assist their American counterparts.

Another difference between domestic and foreign law enforcement was the assistance provided by the JCF was not because of Jamaican statute, but the extent of support was related to the extent of goodwill you could gain from your hosts. I saw this firsthand when I arranged for a trainer from the U.S. Customs Canine Unit to come to the Island and work with my counterparts in the JCF.

I picked him up on Sunday, got him to the hotel, and during dinner, I thanked him for agreeing to come to Jamaica to train the police. The following morning, I picked him up and we drove to the Coast Guard office, where the training would take place. Much to my surprise, when we arrived at the outdoor training facility, there were several tables filled with alcohol and chasers.

The Jamaican Police, always gracious hosts, welcomed us and told us to drink up. A bit startled but not wanting to offend my counterparts, I told them we had not eaten anything and didn't want to drink on an empty stomach. Not missing a beat, the lead police official ordered several jeeps to saddle up. Several vans convoyed to an outdoor restaurant, where we spent the next two hours eating. At the end of the meal, we reentered the vans, returned to the Coast Guard Station, and upon arriving back at our assembly point, my host exclaimed, "Now let's drink."

The mission was eventually completed, although a day later, the Canine Unit received the training. However, we did our part to strengthen the relationship between the two law enforcement agencies.

One anti-drug strategy that was discussed but never implemented was called "crop substitution." The premise of this policy is that you encourage the farmers to cultivate legal farm products in place of the drugs and offset the financial shortfall with money from the government. This policy rarely works because the extremely high profit from manufacturing drugs makes it impossible for the government to match what the traffickers would pay for these services. With all the equipment and technological drawbacks, the Jamaican Police made up with their dedication and spirit. Every request for assistance, manpower, intelligence, and surveillance was immediately acted upon. On a regular basis, American Agents would arrive on the Island and would receive the full assistance of the Jamaican police and military. A typical undercover operation would entail a drug trafficking deal that was arranged in the United States and would call for a pilot to fly a plane onto one of the Island's illegal airfields. Once there the pilot would be met by the Jamaican dealers, who would oversee the loading of the plane with 1,000 to 1,200 pounds of marijuana.

After the loading was completed and the plane taxied off, the police and military would arrest those on the ground. The plane would be tracked by DEA, the U.S. organizers would be arrested in the U.S., and the marijuana would be seized after the plane landed.

We conducted numerous successful investigations of this type. Another strategy we explored was the result of a good working relationship with the U.S. Consulate. Based on an allegation, the consulate informed us they would deny a visa to a Jamaican citizen seeking to enter the U.S.

Consequently, on a regular basis, the consulate would provide us with a list of names for us to check to determine if we had any information that the person was involved in drug trafficking. We would review our files, check with our sources, and provide the consulate with the result of our information.

During one inquiry, we came back with a positive involvement in drugs regarding an allegation. We told the consulate and due to the person's position in the Jamaican Government, we decided to advise the U.S. Ambassador before recommending his visa be denied. The U.S. Ambassador was a former Chairman of the Board for a major farm products company. It was from him I received my first lesson in diplomacy. In addition to being a member of Jamaica's Government, our suspect was also a pilot for the national airline. The political fallout would be immense if the visa of a government official was revoked and this fallout would lead directly to the Ambassador. It's important to note the information we had was not evidence, but an allegation. This would be a powerful move that could have serious negative implications on the relationship between the two governments.

As we sat down to brief the Ambassador, we told him of our information. "Source reporting indicates that Mr. X is involved in the marijuana business." The Ambassador appeared to ponder the statement for a few seconds. He adjusted himself in his seat and he repeated our statements: "Now let's get this straight—you say that Mr. X is a pilot for the national airline, a member of the Jamaican Government, and a marijuana dealer. If I agree to your recommendations and revoke his visa, he loses his job at the airline, he loses his position in the government, and the only job he still has is that of a drug dealer. What's better, a part-time drug dealer or a full-time drug dealer?" A bit confused, I looked at the Ambassador and said, "I never looked at it that way, Mr. Ambassador."

The bottom line was reinforced time and time again—there would not be any strong policy from the U.S. Government encouraging the Jamaican Government to crack down on the dealers. Our effectiveness was the ability to facilitate and develop investigations of American agents. Nineteen eighty-two Jamaica was a drug trafficking paradise: The narcotics unit was severely understaffed, the police were paid poorly, and there were over eighty illegal airfields on the Island. It didn't surprise me to learn that Jamaica became a major transshipment point for cocaine entering the U.S. I've always wondered if "we" would have pushed on the narcotics issue back then, maybe, just maybe, we would have been able to introduce some strong anti-narcotics programs that would have effectively reduced the power and influence of the drug lords. Jamaica is an island paradise and continues to occupy a very special place in my heart.

In less than two years, I was promoted and transferred to Miami. I had mixed emotions about leaving Jamaica. I enjoyed learning and living in a foreign culture. The Jamaican people are extremely intelligent and had welcomed me into their hearts and lives.

CHAPTER 4

Welcome to Miami

Kilogram of Coke and a 9mm

MIAMI IN THE 1980S WAS OUT OF CONTROL. THE COLUMBIAN CARTELS had begun to establish their dominance in the drug world and as is the staple of the narcotics organization, violence was the accepted method of operation. The Medillin cartels had imported ruthless killers to do their business. The daily papers and the local news were filled with headline stories of shootouts at shopping malls and in business districts throughout the city.

The U.S. Government established the South Florida Task Force with combined resources of the Federal Government, DEA, U.S. Customs, and U.S. Coast Guard to operate as a unifying force to stop the importation of cocaine into the U.S. DEA established a task force of agents and homicide detectives to respond to the numerous drug-related murders and coordinate the investigations.

Miami was perceived as a source city for drugs and a feeding ground for U.S.-based organizations distributing cocaine. I had only been out of the country for two years, but the change in drug trafficking was significant. Two years prior in New York City, a good prosecutable case would yield a couple of ounces of cocaine. In Miami, the Untied States Attorney's office had a five-kilogram limit for federal prosecution. What a difference two years made. My impression was that as soon as you landed at Miami International, you were given a kilogram of cocaine and a 9mm and told, "Welcome to Miami." It seemed as if everyone had cocaine and a gun. Not just major drug dealers but low-level dealers and neighborhood criminals could easily get their hands on distribution quantities of cocaine.

Another strategy that DEA Miami deployed was to designate two enforcement groups to assist the agents in the development of their cases. These groups were known as the "Response Groups," and their only responsibility was to assist agents in the development of their cases. The dividing line was the State of Mississippi. One enforcement group was responsible for assisting the offices west of Mississippi, and the other group was responsible for those offices east of Mississippi. I was the supervisor of Enforcement Group 3 (west of Mississippi).

Our typical assignments would be to provide surveillance back up to agents traveling to Miami to meet the drug traffickers and conduct surveillance on residents, and we would also initiate our own cases.

One case involved a lot of ingenuity on the part of the undercover agents. After a series of negotiations that spanned several months, the drug trafficker claimed he could deliver thirty kilograms of cocaine to the undercover agents. It was late in the evening, and we had gone down this road before, so I elected not to take out the money for this alleged drug buy. The agents held a series of meetings with each meeting, supposedly bringing us closer to the thirty kilograms. The trafficker claimed to be able to deliver this night but wanted to be sure we had the money. At this late hour, the administrative personnel had long ago gone home, so even if we wanted to take out the money, we couldn't.

I authorized the agents to use their credit cards and set up the negotiations at high-end hotels and restaurants. To further the undercover role, they were to treat the trafficker to top-shelf food and alcohol. The deal finally came down to the plan for the agents to deliver the money and the cocaine would be released in their possession. We were stuck. Finally, one of the agents suggested we load up a few briefcases with telephone books and tape and lock the briefcases so they could not be easily opened. At the appointed time, the agents carrying the briefcases met the defendant. The visual of the agents carrying the briefcases, which the trafficker assumed was filled with his cash, was enough. The agents walked to the trafficker's car and when he opened the truck, they gave the signal. Two arrests were made, and two duffel bags filled with thirty kilograms of cocaine were confiscated.

Corruption is unfortunately endemic to narcotics enforcement. Some agents who start out with the best training and motives sometimes over time get sloppy and begin to operate in the gray area. When that happens, it's just a matter of time before the agent will get himself in over his head and either get caught outright or someone with whom he/she has committed the criminal act will get arrested and turn on him. I've often wondered what motivates a person in narcotics law enforcement, who knows how the game is played, to commit a drug crime. Knowing that most federal drug investigations will last six to eight months to a year before someone is arrested, how can you ever think you've gotten away clean?

I had a pretty typical group as DEA enforcements groups usually go—some experienced agents and a lot of new agents fresh out of the Academy. The seasoned agents are critical in guiding the new agents in the performance of their duties. The energy and enthusiasm new agents bring to the office is the catalyst that can jumpstart a slow-performing unit.

One experienced agent who worked for me tended to be a lone wolf. He wanted to work undercover by himself with just one backup person. This desire not only didn't make sense to me from a safety point of view, but this practice would also leave him open to allegations by a defendant since the likelihood the surveillance team could corroborate his version of events would be significantly reduced by the lack of appropriate backup.

I remember one day arriving to the office on a Monday morning and meeting this senior agent, who stated very nonchalantly, "Boss, I just wanted to let you know I met with some drug traffickers in a hotel last night." I quickly responded, "How come you didn't call me? If you or anyone in my group is working undercover, I want to know about it. My job is to ensure you have adequate backup." The agent responded by saying, "I don't need close supervision. I've worked undercover hundreds of times. I know what I'm doing. Since you want to over-supervise me, I'm gong to talk to the Special Agent-in-Charge (SAC) and ask him to take me out of your group." I didn't respond but simply walked away. My thoughts were that when he told the SAC he wanted out of my group because I wanted to be advised in advance when an undercover operation was planned, the SAC would definitely support my position. So as the agent walked away, as if he was going to the SAC's office, I felt strong in my decision. Since I never heard from the SAC about a transfer, I considered this matter closed. A few years later this agent was arrested for drug corruption.

Corruption and narcotics trafficking go hand-in-hand. Some agents start out sincere and abiding by the rules and regulations but somehow over time begin to rationalize behavior that compromises their integrity. Since I had just arrived from Jamaica, it was suggested that I help out another federal agency that had information regarding a corrupt employee. I was told that the intermediary, with whom I would meet to discuss the transaction, was a middle-aged man who had never been arrested and had no history of violent behavior. I was to meet with him at his house. Shortly after I arrived at the source's house, a middle aged, non-descript man arrived. As soon as he entered the living room, he put his handbag on the coffee table. I noticed the bag was open and a 9mm was inside. The observation reinforced two things that are the essence of narcotics enforcement: 1) Expect the unexpected, and 2) Money and guns are the tools of the trade.

As a result of the negotiations, I traveled to Jamaica with another DEA agent, acting in an undercover capacity. On the appointed day, we met our trafficker in the bathroom at the Donald Sangster International Airport in Montego Bay, Jamaica.

The trafficker gave us a kilogram of cocaine and told us to go to a certain line, where a U.S. Customs inspector would let us through with the drugs when we arrived at Miami International. We touched down at Miami International and when we went to the prearranged line, the Inspector acknowledged us and let us through without a search or question. He was later arrested and convicted of federal drug violations.

During this time, the State of Florida was awash with large-scale shipments of cocaine coming from South America or washing up on the beaches after having been airdropped in the Bahamas. The resources of the Federal Government and diplomatic efforts were in full force to dent the onslaught.

The U.S. drug policy is shaped by violence. If American citizens are being robbed, assaulted, and killed by drug addicts, the local news will lead the telecast with these stories. The politicians feel compelled to get on their soapbox and legislate new laws or federalize state crimes. The print and electronic media had a lot of graphic stories to tell. The Crime Bill of the 1980s strengthened the government's hand in the battle against the drug lords. For the first time it introduced "truth in sentencing," where convicted defendants would do 85 percent of their prison time, no more time off for good behavior. Also now the only departure from the sentencing guidelines was for cooperation or diminished capacity. The introduction of these laws and expansion of DEA's role overseas led to a slow disintegration of the traditional organized crime groups that dominated the trade in the seventies and early eighties.

DEA had several Administrators by 1986. From my vantage position, the most effective one has been John Lawn. I've always said that when measuring an Administrator, it's not the fact that x amount of drugs or money was seized during his/her watch, but the fact that the "street agent" felt we had a leader who would empower them to "take the hill" and would back them in the event of a controversy.

Jack Lawn was a career FBI executive who became the second FBI agent to lead the DEA. For all the rivalry you hear about DEA and the FBI, Jack Lawn quickly became a strong supporter of the agents and the very dangerous job we did.

In 1982, then President Ronald Regan, with his Attorney General, Edwin Meese, began the process of merging DEA into the FBI. Up until this time, all federal narcotics investigations were conducted solely by DEA with some overlap with U.S. Customs. With seven senior FBI executives occupying the most critical positions in the DEA, the assimilation had begun. At the start, the "Bureau assumed that DEA was a small second-string outfit that couldn't match the talent of the much larger FBI." The more they learned about this new agency, its people, mission, mindset, and culture, there was a realization that not only were these agents up to the task, but they had established a strong record of cooperation with police departments throughout the country and security forces throughout the world. After a few years, it was the consensus of opinion that the American public was well served by a dedicated federal agency whose sole responsibility was narcotics enforcement.

The defining moment of Lawn's tenure and why he has my vote as the best Administrator we've had occurred after the torture and execution of Special Agent Enrique "Kiki" Camerena, who was assigned to the Guadalajara, Mexico Office.

On February 7, 1985, Kiki was kidnapped by drug traffickers as he left the office to meet his wife for lunch. Several days later, his body and that of his source was recovered from a shallow grave. The subsequent investigation, which was spearheaded by Lawn, revealed that Kiki had been beaten and brutally tortured by Mexican traffickers before his death.

Lawn was relentless in his pursuit to identify and arrest all those who conspired to kill Kiki. He handpicked a team of seasoned investigators and removed the bureaucratic barriers that sometimes surface in highly charged investigations. The special operation was know as Leyanda or Lawman. In my book, this was DEA's finest hour— commitment from the top backed up with resources to aggressively support the men and women on the front line. Lawn's strong stance has served notice to vicious international drug traffickers that DEA will use the full resources of the Federal Government to avenge the murder of a drug warrior.

DEA's career path required a tour in Headquarters for further advancement. Since the formation of DEA, the power in the Agency had continually shifted between the Operations Division and the Planning and Inspection Division. As a matter of course, Operations would logically become the focal point and would be the Division with the clout. However, when personalities and egos are involved, logic goes out the window. In the eighties, the Inspection Division had the juice. It was a known fact that those agents on the fast track were sent to the Inspections Division. It became common practice that agents would write the career board requesting an assignment to the Inspections Division. The leader of the unit was a former FBI executive who also became a strong supporter and friend of DEA. He would hand-pick the agents to serve in his division. At the end of a twelve-month tour, he would either promote you or send you to a city you requested. You could imagine my excitement when I was told I had been transferred to the Inspection Division.

Moving is considered one of the principal causes of stress. During the eighties and nineties, the career in DEA required you to move to progress in your career. The prevailing thought, which I agree with, is that the senior leaders would be most effective in their decision making and strategies if they were able to view narcotics enforcement from a variety of assignments, e.g., foreign, domestic, and a tour in Headquarters. Since DEA is an international investigative agency, I believe the most dynamic and effective leaders have viewed this issue from a variety of management experiences.

CHAPTER 5

Headquarters: Washington, D.C.

Where Policy Is Made

DURING THE CHRISTMAS SEASON OF 1986, I MOVED TO WASHINGTON, D.C. After four years in a warm climate, Jamaica and Miami, I had to buy a new winter wardrobe. It's amazing that after a few years, your clothes can quickly go out of style.

Washington, D.C., is the seat of government. The main headquarters for the Drug Enforcement Administration was inside an eight-story building located at 1405 Eye Street, NW. The Inspection Division was located around the corner at 15th and H streets in the Shoreum Building. The Inspection Division was the internal audit and compliance arm of the Agency. As an Inspector, we would travel in teams and review the internal operation of the DEA offices around the world. We would basically issue a report card to the office head after interviewing every employee in the office and the law enforcement contacts within his area of responsibility. Our report was based on three major themes: enforcement operations, administration, and liaison. Our reviews would usually last from two to three weeks with the largest offices, New York, Miami, Los Angeles, Chicago, Houston, Bangkok, Europe, and South America requiring three-week reviews. Needles to say, there has always been a love/hate relationship between the field SAC's and the Office of Inspections.

This assignment was extremely valuable as a primer for a future leader in the DEA. During my fourteen-month tenure in the Inspections Division, we averaged about eight days a month in D.C. We reviewed the internal operations of our offices in New York, Miami, Houston, Chicago, Los Angeles, Bangkok, and Europe (Austria and Germany). All these three-week reviews were in addition to the two-week reviews of medium-sized domestic offices.

At the conclusion of the review the Chief Inspector would fly out from Washington to review the report and lead the closeout with the office head. The stress is built into the process because a bad inspection could result in the removal of the office head and/or his key staff. Consequently, like it or not, all office heads seriously regard the inspection process. During the inspection of the New York Division, I got a chance to reacquaint myself with some old friends. One of them was Special Agent Everett Hatcher, who at the time was one of the senior African-American, non-supervisory agents assigned to the Division.

Late one evening, Hatcher arrived back at the office after returning from home. I asked him what he was doing coming to work at this hour, and he explained that his group was conducting a massive round-up early the following morning, and rather than leave for work extra early and possibly get caught up with the unpredictable New York traffic, it was wiser to travel to the city, spend the night in the office, and be ready to conduct the operation in the early-morning hours. In fact, the New York Division had bunk beds in the gym just for that purpose. The Agents were encouraged to use the bunk beds late at night or early in the morning after a long day of conducting drug investigations.

Hatcher related that he was unhappy with the way the FBI case agents were treating him during the course of this investigation. His frustration was that he was not being told about key aspects of the investigation and was kept in the dark about essential details of the operation. My advice to Hatcher was simple: either stop the undercover work until he was satisfied with the feedback provided by the FBI or agree to train an FBI Agent and introduce him to the suspects with whom he was negotiating. There are usually tensions between the undercover agents and the case agents on the direction of the investigation. These are very high-risk and high-emotion operations where mistakes can be deadly. The best narcotics leaders, though, give full control to the undercover agent during the course of the case. In fact, the best leaders empower the undercover agent to call off the case and abort the deal if they get a sixth sense that something is wrong. The message of empowerment for the undercover agent is one that should be continuously reinforced. We concluded the audit the following week, and when I returned back to D.C. I never realized it would be the last time I saw Hatcher alive. I'll explain this later. Fourteen months later, I was promoted to the position of Deputy Personnel Officer (DPO).

The DPO was a newly established position in an effort to ensure that Personnel, currently referred to as Human Resources, was responsive to the field. The philosophy was to place agents in traditionally non-agent positions. I was the third agent to occupy the position, and it was an experience for me to supervise a primarily non-agent workforce.

The two major programs that impacted on the special agent workforce were Special Agent Recruitment and the Performance Review Grievance Committee, which I chaired.

The Special Agent Recruitment Unit is responsible for overseeing the program and the selection of candidates to attend agent school. Each Domestic Division—there are approximately twenty-two around the country—have a special agent whose full-time job is to recruit potential special agent candidates. The recruitment is usually accomplished by attending college career days and providing student internships. Also, with the numerous criminal justice programs throughout the country, many colleges are aware of the agency and its requirements for selection.

Most law enforcement agencies express their desire to recruit minorities. I submit that the most effective method of increasing the numbers of African-Americans, Hispanics, and women, is to treat these employee groups as valuable members of the organization with a clear and defined career path for them to succeed. If they feel the organization is seriously interested in their success, they will respond in overwhelming numbers and tell others of the fair treatment and career opportunities.

The average time from the submission of the application until the entrance into the Academy is about six months. During this time, there are a lot of opportunities for an applicant to drop out of the system—derogatory information developed during the course of the background investigation, which must be addressed, and credit problems, which must be explained, etc. If the personnel specialist is not closely tracking the candidate, it is very easy for the candidate to fall out of the system. We began to identify weaknesses in the system and stress accountability in the processing of applications. We became focused on increasing the number of minorities entering the Academy and revamping the recruitment program.

One of the senior African-American Special Agents was childhood friends with the V.P. for *Ebony Magazine*. Armed with the inside connection, we traveled to Chicago and met with him and Mr. Johnson, the founder. We told Mr. Johnson of our commitment to increase the number of minorities in the agency.

They gave us the fees for an ad, which would vary depending upon the size, half-page, full-page, etc. Our goal, however, was to maximize the ad by telling the story of a career in DEA from an African-American perspective. This was an education for me, regarding the separation between advertising and editorial. In an effort to preserve the integrity of the magazine, the editorial unit wanted to be independent of the advertising influence, to select stories based solely on their relevance to the target audience. I understand and totally appreciate the philosophy. I also submit that the mission, personnel, and philosophy of DEA is a story that has not been told and has special relevance to those communities infected by drug addicts and the violence perpetrated by drug gangs. We were convinced that the African-American experience in DEA was worthy of an article in an African-American family magazine. So did the owner, John Johnson. Mr. Johnson explained that every August, he produced a special-issue magazine dedicated to a topic of interest to the African-American community. This issue was about the civil right struggle; however, he felt it was important enough to add the drug problem as a special-issue topic. In an effort to capitalize on the reach of *Ebony Magazine* with the African-American community, we selected a husband-and-wife team as our subject for life as a DEA agent. We also designed an ad featuring a male and a female African-American agent with domestic and international experience. Our goal was two-fold: to interest African-Americans in a career in DEA by showing the wide range of assignments and to humanize the Agency with an African-American face. We were able to track a significant increase in African-American interest as a result of the *Ebony* ad.

During my assignment to Headquarters, 1987 to 1989, two watershed events occurred in New York City, which highlighted the dangers of narcotics work.

The first was the murder of Police Officer Edward Byrne, who was executed while guarding a witness in a drug case, and the other was the execution of Special Agent Everett Hatcher, who was killed by a drug dealer who had sold him cocaine. Both of these events crystallized the dangers of narcotics enforcement and the insidious violence perpetrated by drug dealers.

During the 1980s, southeast Queens had emerged as a focal point for crack cocaine distribution. One of the most prolific crack cocaine gangs was led by Pappy Mason and Fat Cat Nicholas. These groups dominated the crack distribution in Queens. A successful investigation by Federal authorities led to the indictment and arrest of the members on federal drug trafficking charges.

Prior to the trial, a police officer was executed while guarding a witness in a drug case. The drug dealers had declared war on the police. The response was swift and forceful. The shooters were arrested and the leaders were prosecuted, convicted, and sentenced to long prison terms.

One of the saddest days in history of the New York Office of DEA occurred on February 28, 1989, when Special Agent Everett Hatcher was murdered by Gus Faraci. Faraci was a low-level mob associate who had recently been released from State Prison, after being convicted of murder. Hatcher, who was working undercover for the FBI, had purchased several ounces of cocaine from Faraci shortly after his release from jail. However, something happened during the course of the investigation that resulted in Faraci's deep suspicion of Hatcher. There is speculation as to what actually caused this suspicion, and it serves no purpose to ponder this issue now. However, from every tragedy is an opportunity for lessons learned. In all undercover narcotics cases, the confidential source is a key to its success. His/her reputation will be the driving force as in whether he/she commands the respect for a long-term investigation or rather a short-term buy-bust case.

Although we will never know for certain why after a meeting, at which no money or drugs were exchanged, Faraci shot Hatcher three times in the head. As Hatcher lay dying seated in the driver's seat of his car, the surveillance team scrambled to find him. The manhunt to catch Faraci, which lasted about twelve months, was a coordinated effort among Federal, State, and Local law enforcement agencies. Yielding to the unrelenting pressure from the New York Law Enforcement Team, the mob ended the manhunt with the execution of Faraci. The message from law enforcement was clear. There would be a dedicated, consistent focus on crime and criminals until we captured Faraci. The criminal element in New York City is well aware of the history of law enforcement's response to a murder of one of their own. Consequently, the track record in New York City is better than 95 percent when it comes to solving the murder of a law enforcement officer killed in the city.

In May of 1989, I was transferred to the Philadelphia Division as the Assistant Special Agent-in-Charge. My responsibility included the drug enforcement operations in Philadelphia; Wilmington; Delaware; Pittsburgh, Pennsylvania; Technical Operations; and Diversion Investigations in the states of Pennsylvania and Delaware.

CHAPTER 6

City of Brotherly Love

Cleaning Up the Badlands

THE PROLIFERATION OF CRACK COCAINE AND THE DRUG ORGANIZATIONS WHO controlled the inner- city distribution with violence became the target of DEA. Philadelphia was the home of several street drug gangs controlled by the Jamaicans and African-Americans.

There was a section of North Philadelphia called the "badlands." This was an area that was completely controlled by the drug gangs who sold their wares with impunity. When President George Bush came to the city for a visit, I, along with the leadership of the Federal, State, and Local law enforcement agencies, gave him a briefing on the drug situation in the city. We had installed a covert camera in the neighborhood and videoed actual drug sales. The scene, which was shot in the morning, graphically depicted the dealers arriving on the scene with a group of about thirty to forty people swarming the area to buy drugs. Quickly, the dealer's assistant arrived and ushered the crowd to line up, single file, in an orderly fashion to buy the drugs. This scenario, which took place in a park, was one that was repeated throughout the nation. We were continuously getting requests from the community to do something to stop the drug dealing. We heard their voices and went into action.

The partnership between an aggressive agent and hardworking prosecutor is unbeatable. The investigative strategy was simple: 1) make undercover drug buys, 2) use covert cameras to record the level of drug dealing, 3) debrief accomplice witnesses, 4) use their testimony for grand jury indictments, and 5) request pretrial detention for the arrested defendants. Philadelphia had a number of open-air markets, where large numbers of people would congregate to buy drugs. The state court system was overwhelmed with offenders charged with a variety of crimes. Consequently, there was a void in the effective investigation and prosecution of neighborhood drug gangs. The task force, composed of representatives from Federal,

State and Local law enforcement agencies, along with the United States Attorney's Office, began to implement a comprehensive strategy, which eventually led to the incarceration of drug gangs and the restoration of public safety to the streets of Philadelphia.

An example of the impact of the strategy occurred during the execution of arrest warrants in the badlands. As the defendants were being handcuffed and placed in the car, they asked whether this was a State or Federal arrest. The word on the street was if you were arrested by the FEDS/DEA, there was no revolving door. The cases were already indicted, and the leaders were authorized by a federal judge to be held on pretrial detention.

The cases were investigated using the full resources of the federal government. The result was a series of cases spanning several years, which led to the arrest and imprisonment of large numbers of drug dealers. Slowly but surely, tranquility was being restored to the streets of Philadelphia.

One group whose drug-dealing organization operated throughout the city was called the Junior Black Mafia (JBM). In a throwback to another era, these men got caught up in the glamour of the street life and were known to wear rings, announcing their membership in the organization with the initials JBM. Through undercover investigation and accomplice witness testimony, this group was eventually put out of business. The electronic and print media had done an outstanding job recording the violence and intimidating power of these organizations. So at the time of sentencing, it was no surprise that the members were sent away for long periods of time. A sentence of twenty years or life imprisonment was not an uncommon prison term.

During the late eighties and early nineties, the sophisticated cartels changed their strategy. Gone was the flash and the outward signs of wealth. The new leaders—Cali Cartel—headquartered in Columbia, operated with the efficiency of CEOs for a Fortune 100 company and the secrecy of a terrorist organization. These organizations had their own attorney's and logistic and marketing experts. They operated with a strong reward-and- discipline system, and they were quite effective as an international criminal organization. Countless times our agents in Bogota, Columbia, would seize records of the major cocaine organizations. These records would detail the biographical information of the members: names of parents, children, and close relatives. When an arrest would occur in the U.S., oftentimes the defendants indicated a desire to cooperate; however, they also knew once their cooperation was known, those family members would be killed. The usual scenario was as soon as the member was arrested, the organization would supply him with an attorney. The attorney was really representing the leaders of the organization by ensuring the arrested member did not cooperate. The strategies employed in drug cases are unique and imaginative.

Drug prevention is a key component of any comprehensive drug strategy. In an effort to enhance our drug prevention program, we partnered with radio station WDAS, E. Steven Collins, program director. The station provided a variety of formats for us to bring our message to the community. Due to the historic tense relationship between the African-American community and law enforcement; community support was instrumental in changing the perception. We had agents appearing regularly on his radio show and we participated in all facets of the station's yearly Community Fair: Unity Day.

As an arm of the Department of Justice, DEA encouraged all its offices around the country to celebrate the various ethnic special programs—African-American History Month and Hispanic and Asian Heritage Month, to name a few. In Philadelphia we began weekly programs during the month of February to celebrate African-American History Month. To enhance the value of the program, we invited students from University City and Overbrook High School to celebrate with us. One memorable program featured Dr. Roscoe Brown as the keynote speaker. Dr. Brown at that time was the President of Bronx Community College; however, he had distinguished himself many years earlier as a Tuskegee Airman, an elite group of African-American pilots who had flown numerous bombing missions during World War II. These hero pilots were noted for their flawless execution. Caught up in the racial climate of their times, this segregated unit was forced to train by themselves and suffered all of the indignities and hostilities from the military.

Dr. Brown, a gifted public speaker, mesmerized these teenagers with a detailed view of the life of an African-American soldier in the military. When he finished his remarks, you would have thought he was a famous rap artist. The teenagers were standing in line, anxiously awaiting their turn to take a picture with him. These scenes, repeated week after week during the month of February, reinforced my belief that if African-American teenagers were taught their history and the many contributions they have made to this society, they would enthusiastically embrace this knowledge. This new awareness would enhance their self-esteem and reinforce their desire to use the obstacles in their lives as opportunities to succeed.

Since I left New York in 1982, I had been promoted several times and was transferred several times. In the winter of 1994, I was promoted and transferred again. Back to the city of my birth, I had mixed emotions. I had enjoyed my assignment in Philadelphia. We put a lot of dangerous, violent drug organizations out of business, but we also gave DEA a face and a voice to the citizens of Philadelphia. The citizens had taken me into their confidence, and I really felt we had put together a superb narcotic enforcement and drug prevention program. Philadelphia will always have a special place in my heart.

CHAPTER 7

Corruption: The Elite New York Drug Enforcement Task Force Takes a Hit

IN NOVEMBER 1993, I REPORTED TO THE TASK FORCE FOR A ONE-WEEK TDY assignment. The Special Agent in Charge, Bob Bryden, was aware of my previous assignment in New York. He invited me back to reacquaint myself with my New York contacts and spend time with him in an effort to learn his management style and become aware of the "hot button" issues in the office. I had a great week. I was excited about coming home, and I felt fortunate to work for Bob. Although he had recommended an executive in the New York Office for the task force job, he was one of the first callers to congratulate me and welcome me to the management team in New York.

The person I was replacing had to retire because he had reached the mandatory retirement age of fifty-seven. He had been in New York City the majority of his career except for a brief assignment in Washington, D.C. He was one of those managers who would have stayed forever, whether or not his effectiveness had diminished. Although he had to retire in a few months, he had made no post-DEA plans.

On Monday morning, I reported to the New York office, located at 10th Avenue and 17th Street. I proceeded to the eighth floor to meet with Bob Bryden. Bob gave me an overview of the division and the task force and told me to enjoy myself this week:, to spend some time reestablishing old ties and becoming familiar with the division. I left his office excited about my new challenge, and headed downstairs to the task force. Since the division was undergoing an inspection, I headed to the back of the office to get an assessment from the inspectors as to their view of the operation. As I headed through the door, I reversed myself and decided to meet with the outgoing leader of the task force. Protocol dictated that my first meeting with task force staff should be with the incumbent. As I entered the front office, I greeted John and told him when he had some time, I'd like to sit down and talk with him. John was seated at his desk, writing. He looked up at me with a fleeting glance and waved his hand. He stated that he was too busy and would not have any time to talk with me.

I felt embarrassed but not deterred. I was acutely aware that any time you are an African-American in a highly visible or first-time position, things are not going to be easy. My initial reaction was to go toe to toe with him; however, I left with a smile on my face, my head up, and a determination that my promotion to this very important assignment would remain a positive sign of my accomplishments and an opportunity to advance the mission of the New York Drug Enforcement Task Force.

During this time, the relationships among the DEA, the NYPD, and the NYSP were extremely fragile. Three members of the NYDETF (two detectives and one state trooper) were arrested and charged with narcotic violations. They had been caught stealing drugs and giving them to an informant to sell. They had also used their inside knowledge of investigations, gleaned from wiretaps, to rob drug dealers and raid stash houses. These were very dangerous people. Their exploits were thwarted by a very honest and mission-oriented former lieutenant of the NYPD, Jim Wood.

Narcotics work is very dangerous business. Double crossing, lies, and death are the underpinning of undercover investigations. In the instant case, an informant who is working with the agency, introducing his former associates in the underworld to federal agents for eventual arrest and prosecution, now has to make a decision that may get him killed. Law enforcement officers, on whom he relies for payment and his personal safety, have now crossed the line and are giving him drugs (heroin) to sell. What should he do? If he decides to turn them in, to whom? He could turn them in to somebody who is aware and condones this illegal operation. How high up is the knowledge of this drug dealing? Is the corruption limited to these officers only, or are others involved in these deals? The wrong decision could get you killed. Should you just go along with what these "officers" have requested you do? You're a drug dealer. Now you're dealing for the cops? The informant reached out for a man who he knew was honest with the utmost integrity and as straight as an arrow, (NYPD) Lieutenant Jim Wood.

Wood immediately made the proper notifications, and an investigation was launched, which resulted in the arrest of Beck, Termini, and Roibles on federal drug charges.

There were some who felt since the NYDETF was headquartered with DEA, the agency protected their own agents, who should also have been arrested. Anytime a law enforcement official is arrested, the unit they are assigned to comes under intense pressure as the agency leaders attempt to vigorously determine who else is involved in criminal activity. The NYPD's response was swift: massive numbers of detectives were automatically transferred out of the NYDETF. In an environment like this, rumors take on added weight, and the careers of a lot of good men and women are put on hold and in some cases ruined.

The NYDETF had always been considered the best off-duty assignment in the NYPD. Now the jewel had been tarnished. This organization, which had withstood the changes in D.C.'s politics and personalities, was now on the verge of a break-up.

When I arrived, there had been a series of changes enacted in the task force, which resulted in tighter controls. The agents felt these new procedures indicated a severe lack of trust and that since narcotic work was not an exact science, maybe it was better not to be proactive and to simply show up each day and go through the motions. They were further annoyed that several additional levels of supervision were added to their normal operations. For example, newly established procedures enacted after the arrests required a NYPD lieutenant or DEA ASAC to be on the scene during the execution of a search warrant. The agents believed that this policy was unnecessary and it basically reduced the authority of the first line supervisor, especially since this was a rule that was not applied to any other DEA unit, solely the NYDETF.

The first six months were spent increasing the communication flow among the leadership of the task force. We held regular meetings with the supervisors, where investigations were discussed. Top management became aware of impediments, and it also allowed us to compliment the men and women for the important and dangerous work they were undertaking—without public recognition—for the citizens of this great country.

We created an award corner, where task force awards were prominently displayed for all members to see. We also scheduled in-service and motivational training for the members. The topics included integrity, testimony, and special operations. Pat Riley, then the head coach of the New York Knicks, spoke about leadership and adjusting to change. George Keiling, author of *Broken Windows*, which was the blue print for the NYPD's concentration on quality of life crimes, spoke about law enforcement and it's relationship to crime reduction. John O'Neill, deceased, former Special Agent in Charge of the FBI's New York office, spoke about international terrorism and its nexus to international drug trafficking.

These efforts were designed to recreate the esprit de corps, which is essential to a successful narcotics enforcement unit. It didn't happen overnight, but we soon rebounded with a renewed sense of teamwork and the thrill of successful investigations.

There is no narcotic investigative unit in the country that operates with the energy, enthusiasm, and intensity of the New York Division. On any given week, because of the competitive spirit and talent of the members, million-dollar seizures, thousands of kilograms of heroin and cocaine, and the arrest of major international drug dealers occur throughout the world, based on task force cases.

Along with this focused level of enforcement is ever present danger. During my tenure as the leader of the task force and as the Special Agent in Charge we faced two situations where shots were fired and the defendants died.

Police work is not an exact science. In narcotics work, where guns, violence, and betrayal are the essence of the trade, every encounter with a suspect can result in death. To be successful in narcotics work, you have to be aggressive and disciplined and fine-tune the ability to expect the unexpected. I've watched with interest as the New York media second guesses law enforcement officers when shots are fired and defendants are killed. Having been involved in a shooting myself, I know firsthand of the fear, anxiety and uncertainty law enforcement officers experience when they fire their weapon and take a life.

The media has the luxury of dissecting frame by frame a deadly encounter that took place in seconds, whether the suspect displayed a weapon or what appeared to be a weapon or whether the officer can effectively articulate what he saw or thought he saw that caused him to fire his weapon. These issues may determine whether the officer/agent faces administrative sanctions and/or criminal penalties. The call that every law enforcement leader dreads is: "We've had a shooting."

At approximately 5:00 a.m., I received a call from Joy, our young female radio operator, regarding a shooting that had taken place in the Bronx. Her voice steady and firm, awakened me with the words: "Mr. Rice, I just received a report from T-11 (code name for the supervisor of task force group 11). Shots fired and the perp is dead. No other injuries." Her tone did not reveal the seriousness of the situation. Joy began to hang up, realizing the severity of her message, I excitedly asked, "where are they now? Have T-11 call me ASAP." Shortly after I spoke to the supervisor, I advised Washington of the situation and told them I was responding to the scene and I would call them when I got on site.

When I arrived on the scene, the block was barricaded with police. The defendant was still lying on the floor as crime scene technicians and the detectives collected evidence. As the picture of events that had taken place earlier became clearer, we advised our Office of Chief Counsel in Washington of the facts, and we requested Department of Justice representation for the NYPD Sergeant and detective who were involved in the shooting.

The team had knocked on the door, identifying themselves as law enforcement officers. The defendant proceeded to open the door. As the team began to enter, he attempted to close the door. A confrontation occurred. The defendant ran into a back room, the team in pursuit. As the team entered the back room, he turned completely around and ran toward the team. The team fired several shots, and the defendant died on the spot.

Although the defendant did not have a gun, the team was able to effectively articulate the facts and circumstances that led to the shooting. The grand jury heard the evidence and ruled the shooting justified. This was considered a noteworthy event in the annuals of the NYPD's relationship with the Bronx. The police shot and killed unarmed Hispanic male in his house, and the citizens of the Bronx ruled it justified.

In the drug world, there are groups that specialize in robbing drug dealers. These are very dangerous people who are willing to take the risks—life and death risks—to acquire money. They are aware of the ruthlessness of their prey and come prepared to steal the drugs and money and even kill innocent people in the process. Occasionally, we would receive information about a specific groups plan to steal drugs. In order to convince a federal prosecutor this was not a mere case of entrapment, where we were encouraging the drug robbery gang to commit the crime, we would conduct a detailed background investigation on the group to include prior arrests and convictions. We would also establish the group had done these drug robberies before and this was their specialty; drug robberies.

We would create a scenario that would allow the drug robbery gang the opportunity to commit the robbery. Once inside, the Emergency Service Unit (ESU) of the NYPD would secure the location so the arrests and seizures could take place. ESU is the highly trained, motivated, and specialized unit of the NYPD. This is the unit that the cops and DEA agents call when they need assistance. On numerous occasions, with no vested interest in the outcome of the case, based on a telephone call, the members of ESU gladly volunteered to employ their tactics to ensure safety for the public and the law enforcement team.

One of the special things about New York is the support we receive from the business community. The Federal Law Enforcement Foundation (FLEF), headed by Tony Bergamo and Zane Tankel, consistently provided support to the men and women of Federal, State, and Local law enforcement agencies throughout the country. Their support includes financial assistance in time of tragedy, illness, and support to at-risk teenagers in the city. On the strength of a telephone call, the FLEF sponsored a private reception for about two dozen members of ESU who had assisted us in several dangerous investigations. The event, held at Morton's in midtown, lasted for several hours with shrimp appetizers, steak and lobster, fine wine, and top-shelf liquor. The evening was topped off with complimentary cigars for those inclined to smoke.

When you look at the cooperation and support among the investigative agencies in New York, that spirit is fostered by the goodwill generated by the FLEF.

CHAPTER 8

DEA Detroit: A Division on the Move

IN APRIL 1996, I WAS PROMOTED TO THE POSITION SPECIAL AGENT IN Charge (SAC) Detroit Division. At forty-three, I was the youngest SAC in the country. DEA divides the U.S. and the Caribbean into twenty-two regions, each region headed by the Special Agent in Charge. I was responsible for the federal drug enforcement and prevention programs throughout the states of Michigan, Ohio, and Kentucky.

Detroit was a city poised for a revitalization. After the riots of the 1960s, businesses that were destroyed or displaced never returned. In essence, a vibrant downtown, which is essential to the life and character of a city, was missing. Outside of "Greek town," an area of boutiques, shops and restaurants, major commercial establishments were missing. There were no department stores, cineplexes, or malls to attract visitors. With the advent of casino gambling and new baseball and football stadiums, the infrastructure is being created to encourage tourism and stabilize downtown.

The office was going through racial turmoil. The SAC, who was white, and his deputy, who was black, were constantly fighting. Unfortunately, when you have this line up, the effectiveness of the office is diminished and the citizens lose. I wasn't told about these problems when I was selected; however, as I began to talk to key DEA headquarters components, it became apparent there were major problems. Fortunately, I was able to select several deputies and firstline supervisors who had distinguished reputations for fairness and leadership. As is usually the case, there are two sides to every story. The former SAC had made several bad management decisions that impacted negatively on African-American agents. The deputy, instead of attempting to resolve these issues, would encourage the employees to file a grievance. This served him well, since he too had filed a grievance against the SAC. DEA Headquarters had sent a team to conduct interviews and make recommendation as to culpability. The result of the investigation was the SAC was out and I was in—on my way to Detroit.

Once in Detroit, I quickly began to build my management team, and meet with the agents in the office and the law enforcement team in the state: FBI, ATF, Detroit PD, Secret Service, Michigan State Police, etc. I soon found out I had inherited an office of people who wanted to work and contribute to the mission of the DEA. I also learned that since Detroit was in close proximity to the much larger Chicago Division, the accomplishments of the agents/officers were often overshadowed by the Chicago office. Slowly building my management team, I made sure we were selecting quality people for our supervisory positions. We also began to revitalize a dormant public relations program. I selected a sharp, energetic agent for the full-time position of Public Information Officer, Durell Hope.

We contacted the *Detroit Free Press* and arranged for an interview, where I had an opportunity to introduce myself to the citizens of Detroit. We also held an open house to introduce the law enforcement community to my management team. Within sixty days of my arrival, I had selected a dozen new agents to key positions.

Under the philosophy of rewarding in public and disciplining in private, we held an awards ceremony at which the Mayor of the City, Dennis Archer, spoke and took pictures with the awards recipients. Art Lewis, former Acting Deputy Administrator, DEA and my mentor came to Detroit to introduce me to his contacts to ensure that I received a warm welcome.

The Executive Deputy Police Commissioner, Benny Napoleon, and I were around the same age. Benny was also very much respected in the Detroit community. Every time I found myself at a community event or gathering of the citizens of Detroit, Benny would go out of his way to inform the group that although I was not from Detroit, I had the wellbeing of the citizens and children first and foremost in my heart. For an executive who is not from the area, an endorsement from a respected leader certified that I was okay. Everywhere I went in the city, people pulled out the red carpet for me. Benny, I thank you. Your support allowed me to quickly gain the confidence of the citizens of Detroit and the Detroit PD. This was no easy feat. Several police commanders told me stories of the former mayor's distrust of the feds. To this extent, any police officer found to be working with the federal investigative authorities would have his career quickly derailed.

We held a three-day supervisors conference to build morale. It is my belief that every progressive organization has a moniker or mantra that quickly sums up its mission. Ours was "DEA Detroit: A Division on the Move." We created hats, coffee mugs, pens, etc., with this logo. It became our motto.

The key to any successful drug enforcement program is prevention-treatment and enforcement. The primary responsibility of DEA is enforcement. Overall, DEA does an extremely effective job in the identification, investigation, and arrest of major narcotic dealers. All of our offices have an agent assigned to coordinate our drug prevention strategy. In Detroit, under the vision of Faye Baker, then principal of Hubert Elementary School, we were able to provide support to the school's prevention program. My tenure in Detroit was the shortest of my career: eleven months. I was promoted to the SAC position in New York State. I've come full circle.

DEA
US

Federal Law Enforcement Foundation Award Luncheon at the Waldorf Astoria. October 27, 2005

With the Philadelphia Law Enforcement team as I brief President George Bush on the drug situation in Philadelphia. 1992

With Art Lewis, former Deputy Administrator of the Drug Enforcement Administration - 1998. The highest ranking African-American in DEA and my mentor.

Lew Rice, January 1975 at the DEA Training in Quantico, Virginia.
22 years old.

Philadelphia Division award ceremony honoring Radio Station WDAS for all their anti-violence and drug prevention programs. 1990. Left to Right: Me, E. Steven Collins, Thera Martin Connely, Tamlin Henry, and Sam Billbrough

Me and Special Agent Dwight Raab at a retirement party. Let the good times roll.

CHAPTER 9

New York Division: It's Not Over until We Win

ON WEDNESDAY, MARCH 12, 1997, I REPORTED TO THE NEW YORK DIVISION as the Special Agent in Charge. In fact, I reported a few days ahead of schedule. I was extremely excited about coming home to sit in the big chair. The New York Division is the flagship of the agency. New York is the media capital, business capital, fashion capital, and the headquarters for the major criminal organizations that operate throughout the world.

The enforcement program had changed dramatically since I had begun my career on the streets of New York City over twenty years ago. Back then the leaders of the drug organization resided in New York City and were akin to celebrities. The media would photograph them at the Copacabana, enjoying a show, or Madison Square Garden, watching a fight. They also believed they were immune from significant prosecutions. However during the 1980s, with the enactment of the Federal Organized Crime Control Bill, that changed. Now minimum mandatory sentences were established based on the amount of drugs purchased, seized or, in the case of conspiracy cases, distributed during the course of the conspiracy.

The methods of investigation had dramatically changed. Twenty years ago, the undercover agent was essential in gaining insight into the criminal organizations planning. Today most high-level drug dealers refuse to meet anyone new unless they know your family members and where they live. Wiretaps are essential in acquiring critical information and evidence, which will lead to the arrest and prosecution of the upper echelon drug dealers on federal drug trafficking charges.

Secrecy and selected violence are critical to the success of these major drug organizations. Compartmentalization is the hallmark of their business. The cocaine cowboys of the eighties have been replaced by the business savvy and acumen of today's drug dealers. Countless times we've seized ledgers with application forms for membership, instructions on where to buy your house, naming what social clubs and organizations to join and type of cars to purchase. Never do anything that calls attention to yourself—blend in.

The leadership has learned their lessons well. It is any wonder that on the day of the arrest, when neighbors are seen in handcuffs, there is a collective response of disbelief? No one ever imagined this "perfect" family could be involved in the sale of illegal drugs.

As I began my new assignment, I felt I was well prepared for the challenge. My past professional experience and knowledge of the city would enable me to move quickly to fine tune the operation and ensure we made it extremely tough for major dealers to operate.

You cannot fully discuss the drug situation in America without dealing with the issue of race, be it the federal crack cocaine laws, which establish minimum-mandatory prison sentences for five to ten grams of cocaine with a 100 to 1 equivalent for powder cocaine. Anecdotal evidence suggests that African-American drug of choice is crack and White Americans' is powdered cocaine.

On one hand, the minority community expects law enforcement to prevent crime but also distinguish between the criminals and those who are simply enjoying their neighborhood. This is where leadership plays a significant role in the quality of enforcement a community will receive. If the law enforcement leader winks and provides blanket support for the team regardless of the circumstances, things can go wrong quickly. Most law enforcement officers are intelligent and aggressive and want to protect the innocent and arrest the criminals. With good leadership, effective supervision, and training, they are poised to gain respect and admiration of the people they serve.

When I took over the New York Division, I set a clear tone that if you made an honest mistake in the performance of your duty, I would back you 100 percent. However, if due to negligence or inattention you made a mistake, you must be ready to deal with the consequences. Because we have guns, carelessness on our part could have deadly consequences for the citizens.

Narcotics trafficking had blossomed during the last twenty years. Money laundering became a special operation whereby small denominations of cash were collected from drug organizations to be deposited in bank accounts, brokerage firms, etc., and then wired to financial institutions around the world. As a full-service agency, as the drug traffickers shifted strategies, we also adjusted ours.

In the late 1990s, we joined with the U.S. Customs Service to coordinate an undercover money laundering operation. Agents advertised their ability to take in large amounts of cash and deposit it for disbursements.

In the instant scenario, we arranged to meet a defendant to take possession of a quarter-million dollars. Unbeknownst to us, the money launderers we were scheduled to meet were being followed for an eventual rip-off.

They traveled from Queens to meet us at the McDonald's parking lot in Manhattan to transfer the money. Trailing them we later found out was a group of ten to fifteen drug dealers with guns who were waiting for the right moment to steal a quarter-million dollars.

As they entered the parking lot, located at 10th Avenue and 34th Street, we watched in anticipation as our undercover agents picked up the money. However, as echoed and reinforced in the training academy, "expect the unexpected" as the defendants' car arrived and parked, agents stationed inside the McDonald's Restaurant watched as the undercover agent went over to the money car.

Shots rang out. A customs agent was hit, one defendant was shot dead, and several were arrested in the lot. A "routine" undercover assignment, where we were to pick up money, quickly developed into a deadly confrontation with the seizure of a quarter-million dollars in cash, several arrests, one defendant dead at the scene, and a customs agent shot.

This scenario reinforced the message that every interaction with drug dealers could end violently. It also reinforced the wisdom of always having adequate manpower on the street. We spent the next twenty-four hours dealing with the media, searching for the defendants who had escaped, and ensuring that the wounded agent was receiving quality medical treatment. The press surrounded the hospital and were demanding a statement. My U.S. Customs counterpart wanted to downplay the shooting and not give a statement since this incident was connected to an international investigation. However, it became obvious that in the city of New York, with these facts—Federal Agent shot, a quarter-million dollars seized, one defendant dead, three in custody, and all this activity taking place in the parking lot of a McDonald's Restaurant in Manhattan—it would be impossible to downplay. Later that evening, we gave a statement to the media, updating the public on the events that had recently transpired.

When I began my career, the veteran agents would socialize with the junior agents by telling them stories of heroism and bravery. The stories introduced us to the legacy of narcotics work: undercover, surveillance and conspiracy investigations. My first supervisor, Frank, was a great storyteller and ensured that the oral history of narcotics agents was passed on to the next generation of agents. One of the early drug cases in the predecessor agency to DEA, the Bureau of Narcotics and Dangerous Drugs, led to the early deaths of two respected veteran agents. In 1972 Frank Tumillo and Tom Devine were involved in a shootout at a hotel in the city. Frank was the undercover agent, and Tom was part of the surveillance team located in an adjacent hotel room. Arrangements were made for the defendants to come to the hotel room to count the money in anticipation of a major drug purchase. Once this occurred, the defendants would leave and return with the heroin. However, when the defendants entered the room, they immediately started firing their weapons. Frank was shot and died on the spot. Tom entered the undercover room from the adjoining room and was immediately shot and remained paralyzed as a result of his wounds. Ten years later, Tom died. When you read the report of the shooting, one quickly realizes this scenario could happen today.

Twenty-five years later, despite numerous advances in technology, training, and equipment, undercover work is still extremely dangerous. We plan to acquire evidence and effect an arrest. However, the drug dealers have their own plan. The drug dealers can plan to injure, murder or kidnap you. We are always in a reactive mode.

In 1997, we formally named the training room the Tumillo and Devine Training Room. Deputy Administrator Jim Milford, along with Tom's wife and kids and Frank's father, sister, and close friends, celebrated with us on this special day. We reinforced to the family of these two American heroes that the law enforcement profession is a special profession. Twenty-five years after their loved ones were killed in the line of duty, we didn't forget our fallen brothers. This was a message not only to the grieving families but also to the present-day agents that you belong to a special organization steeped in pride and tradition. Carry it on.

I've always believed that undercover work is a very special occupation filled with men and women who just want to make a difference. They join this profession to simply help their fellow citizens. It's important these men and women who put themselves into harm's way each and every day receive support and effective leadership from those who are fortunate to lead them. They deserve no less.

The most effective drug strategy must address three key areas: enforcement, prevention, and treatment. At DEA, our primary mission is enforcement; however, because of the vision of our former leaders, DEA's demand reduction program was formulated. In each of DEA's domestic field offices, there are agents whose primary responsibility is to partner with local police, community and private sector groups, and manage the agency's drug prevention program. Twenty-five years on the front line of the "drug war" taught me that at a fundamental level, young people will, at some time in their lives, have to make a choice of whether or not to use drugs. Today's young people are as bright and adventurous as their parents were in their teen years. With the advent of the internet, knowledge is just a click away. Credible information, not scare tactics, will aid a young persons understanding of the dangerous chances they take with their lives when they use an illicit substance. However, the traffickers—students of American culture— have dramatically changed their marketing techniques.

When I was buying heroin on the streets of New York City over twenty-five years ago, personal use and wholesale amounts of heroin ran anywhere from 2 percent to 8 percent. The primary method of ingestion was through intravenous injection. In the mid- nineties, the Columbian cartel expanded the cultivation of opium and began producing for export, high-quality heroin. As HIV and AIDS awareness grew, no longer was the needle the preferred method for drug ingestion. The production and quality of heroin was dramatically increased to allow for the "snorting" of heroin to obtain a high. During my time in New York, we conducted studies with teenage addicts who told us that even though they were snorting heroin every day, they did not consider themselves addicts. Their picture of an addict was someone who stuck a needle in his arm and walked around aimlessly every day. Also, the image of the man in the raincoat standing outside the school offering the kids drugs had changed. This generation, whose parents want them to live better than they did, myself included, sometimes shower them with too much money and idle free time. The teenager who experiments with and introduces others to drugs is likely to be the class president or the captain of a sports team.

The cartels have also regrouped and for the last few years have been flooding American cities with ecstasy, or X. It is produced in western Europe in a pill form at a price of fifty cents per pill. Ecstasy is shipped by air, land, and sea in bulk lots. It's a psychedelic drug with stimulant properties, usually ingested at the rave clubs, where techno music is played. It produces a euphoric effect, where hugs and a desire to touch are often displayed, hence ecstasy's other name: the love drug.

In a dance club in Miami, New York City, or Los Angeles, the price increases from $25.00 to $40.00 a pill. Is there any wonder why so many young people are willing to take the chance and become involved in the illegal drug trade, importation, distribution? Primary distribution takes place inside the club and not the street; hence, monitoring these sales had become problematic but not impossible for law enforcement.

Joining with the NYPD, we made several significant arrests of major ecstasy dealers.

One of the deadly side-effects of ecstasy is the rapid rise of body temperature. You overheat and consume large amounts of water to prevent dehydration. The club owners, aware of the physical effects of ecstasy, have taken to shutting off the water in the bathroom and charging astronomical prices for bottled water. Another step in this unholy arrangement: The club owner will allow dealers to sell drugs in the club for a percentage of the profits.

What a wakeup call for parents. Your teenage son or daughter wants to go to the teen club. The club advertises on the radio that it doesn't sell alcohol on "teen night." A big smile comes across your face and you quickly say yes. You even volunteer to drive your child to the club, not realizing you may just as well be driving your child to a "crack house," a place where drugs are easily purchased and consumed.

The penalties for ecstasy were synonymous with the marijuana laws. To change this and educate the public on the new threat teenagers faced, DEA launched a major campaign of ecstasy awareness. In June 2000, I testified before the House subcommittee on narcotics about the effect of ecstasy, why the penalties should be increased, and the cunning and ingenuity of this new breed of trafficker.

The difficulty we faced was that there was not a poster child for the new drug. In a media-driven society, unless there is violence—murder, assaults, or kidnappings— associated with the drug, or an overdose involving a celebrity, the media will not focus its lights on the issue.

Our strategy was to engage the community and private sector groups. We launched an initiative with the partnership for a drug-free America as they unveiled a new set of ads to address this new drug of abuse.

We also formed a partnership with Waldlegh High School in Harlem. *Emerge Magazine* had featured the story of Kemba Smith. Kemba was a college student at Hampton University, a girl from a middle-class family, who got involved with the wrong crowd. Can you imagine the heartbreak of her parents? You send your young, innocent, naïve daughter to college. She falls in love with the wrong guy, a drug dealer. He gets arrested, she gets arrested. The drug is crack, enter the federal minimum mandatory sentencing guidelines where the only departure from the guidelines are if you cooperate or can prove mental incapacitation. Your naïve daughter probably knew her boyfriend was not a CEO of a Fortune 500 Company; however, since he somehow hid the extent of his drug dealing from her, she didn't ask the tough questions. She gets pregnant, he gets killed. She had no one to cooperate against, so she goes to federal prison for fifteen years. This is a parents nightmare.

The old DEA had spent many years in Harlem—Nicky Barnes, Frank Lucas, Big Robbie Steppeny, all major narcotic dealers who made Harlem their stomping ground. With the advent of the international cartels replacing the French connection, the leaders of the major organizations remain inside foreign countries and communicate with their members through cell telephones, computers, faxes, and pagers.

We decided to return to Harlem and work with the students. The principal and teachers welcomed us with open arms. At an assembly program we, me and four agents, were introduced to a group of twenty students. The teacher introduced us, saying, "We're going to hear from Special Agents from the Drug Enforcement Administration." To our surprise, several students got up and walked out. We introduced ourselves and took turns extolling the students on the value of a drug-free lifestyle. For the next two hours, we had a heated discussion on their interactions with the police, usually negative, their opinions of the drug war, and the lack of opportunities for African-Americans to legitimately earn a living in the society. These teenagers were extremely bright and articulate. They were able to passionately express themselves. It was at this session that I first heard the term "playa haters." One student constantly referred to us as playa haters. He also made a statement to me that would stick in my mind for years to come: "You mean, you can actually go home and sleep at night after arresting a drug dealer?" It was an easy answer; however, that this bright, young African-American student could identify with the drug dealer and see us as the enemy troubled me. We had a lot of work to do.

We left the school and went to get something to eat. On the way to the restaurant and during our meal, we shared our disappointment and concern. We were African-American males working in an agency that was not always supportive to African-Americans; however, we continued to pursue our careers to always ensure that the federal governments drug strategy was fair and balanced, that the targets of investigation were appropriate and those selling drugs were removed from the community. We are the good guys. We must do a better job of informing the public—our young people—telling them who the real heroes are.

Although our fist reaction was we'll stay downtown where we received a degree of respect, that feeling only lasted until our meal was served and collectively we said these are our kids. If they don't make it, we don't make it. We're going back. This time we asked Loretta Lynch, who at that time was the Deputy United States Attorney and later the United States Attorney for the Eastern District of New York. We wanted to show the students a successful African-American female operating at the highest levels of the federal criminal justice system. Usually, a more junior attorney would make this presentation. However, I knew Loretta's dedication was not merely as a supervisory prosecutor but also as an educator who, because of her intellect and demeanor, would quickly connect with the students.

Loretta didn't hesitate. A week later, we were back at the school. Loretta carefully explained the federal aiding and abetting statute. By merely referring someone to another person to buy drugs, you could be charged in a federal narcotic conspiracy if the sale occurs. The students asked a lot of questions and we had a very productive session.

In New York City, the media always exacerbates the exchanges between the police and the African-American community. Law enforcement is not seen as an occupation that is desirable for African-Americans. However, the opportunity to really make a difference in the life of the community, to free a community from the scourge of drugs, is a worthy cause.

In October 1999, I became eligible to retire from the DEA after twenty-five years of service. My previous assignment to Detroit three years earlier had been a very traumatic experience for my daughter Rochelle. She had been enrolled in four different schools in the last eight years, all before seventh grade. While in Detroit, I promised her that the high school she started would be the one from which she graduated. The friends she would make in high school I felt would be very important to her emotional development. I also caught a glimpse of how disruptive these transfers could be to a teenager when we selected a school for her in Detroit. Karen and I took her to the school to get a feel for the neighborhood. As luck would have it, the principal was there. She held her hand, took her around the school, and explained the upcoming curriculum and activities at the school. In spite of this warm welcome from the principal, the day before school started, she told me she couldn't sleep. I asked her why, and she said she didn't know. She just couldn't go to sleep. I immediately sensed she was nervous. She was going to another new school. Were the kids going to like her? Was she going to like them? Right then, I made my decision that although I love my job, when I became eligible, I would retire and take a job in the private sector.

CHAPTER 10

Transition: Life after DEA

JANUARY 31, 2001. AFTER TWENTY-SIX YEARS AND THREE MONTHS, I OFFICIALLY retired from DEA. I had made up my mind about eighteen months prior that I would retire. I had moved seven times in fifteen years. Although all of the moves were either due to promotion or my volunteering, I had made a promise to my daughter that the high school in which she started would be the one from which she graduated. All throughout my career, I had seen effects on the families of agents when they transferred to cities, domestic and overseas. They had to uproot their teenage children and move to places where they had no friends, family, or support system. Mom or Dad would report to the new assignment with a strong familiarity for the culture and job requirements and would dig in and learn the office politics and law enforcement issues. This usually happened while working twelve-hour days while the family was left alone to acclimate to the new neighborhood and school system and develop friends. Many agents either passed up on the promotion or struggled with the stress of families not adjusting to the new move. During the early years of DEA, the motto was: "If DEA wanted you to have a wife, they would have issued you one." Not a family friendly philosophy.

Once you became a Special Agent In Charge (SAC), the feeling was not if you will go back to Washington, D.C., but when. So once I became eligible to retire, I had made up my mind that I would. I was the SAC of the largest operational office in the world and the first African-American to hold that position. Also in the back of my mind was a conversation I had with the Administrator when he asked me to take a position in Washington. My response was since I couldn't retire, if my paycheck went to D.C., I would have to follow but without my family. Administrator Donny Marshall, who's a decent man, let me stay in New York but told me this guarantee was not forever. With this as a backdrop, I was ready to join my peers with a leadership job in the private sector.

Pete O'Neill, a very successful businessman, who is considered the guru for those in law enforcement entering the private sector, took me under his wing and became my mentor. He gave me some very valuable tips on compensation issues, marketing, resume writing, and interviewing. Pete is a former law enforcement officer who left after ten years and became a strong advocate for law enforcement officers entering Corporate America—guys like me, have spent a lifetime doing the "right thing" on behalf of the citizens for no other reason other than it was the right thing to do, not for fame or fortune. Consequently, it's awkward for us to discuss salary, benefits and enter the job market.

I must admit after a career of asking questions and having people respond, it was extremely humbling presenting myself as a prospective job applicant. I hadn't had a job interview in over twenty-five years.

During the interview sessions, the questions always came down to this: "Mr. Rice, you have a impressive background. How do we know you're not going to get bored after a few months? We don't have any issues here that will match the excitement you experienced at DEA." My answer was simple. After having been assigned to all the drug hot spots around the world, I had enough excitement and stories to last me a lifetime. If I were looking for similar excitement, I would be applying for law enforcement jobs. That chapter in my life is closed.

Organizations, public or private, survive on their ability to get time-sensitive information. The old adage "information is power" applies in a post 9-11 world. If you take a look at most companies, the only person who can call the leadership at a law enforcement agency and get answers is the Chief Security Officer. If you've hired the right person, he/she has the contacts and respect to deliver.

I'll never forget the day I had a conversation with a senior executive in the corporate sector on the need for pre-employment screening. His response was since we hire people who are highly intelligent and proactive, there is no need for this. My response was, at your position in the company, you should believe you're hiring the best people but how do you know that if you don't do pre-employment screening? He looked at me like I had two heads. Fast forward to 9-11. I ran into this same executive in the hallway and I said to him, "Those nineteen highjackers were highly intelligent and proactive." He never responded but quickly moved on.

One thing you quickly learn in private security is that since security is not the main focus of the business, you very rarely have enough resources: people and money. In some respects, this is the same in government. The true leader is able to surpass expectations in spite of this drawback.

Case in point: We had a break-in at one of the offices in midtown. We were co-located with several other businesses. Fortunately, we had a closed-circuit TV that recorded the suspect breaking onto the floor and stealing a laptop. After reviewing the tape, I noted a few things that stood out: 1) When this person entered the floor, he never turned on the lights, usually the first thing you do when you enter a dark room. 2) Although the lights were off, you could see he was wearing a hoodie with large symbols on the front. 3) From the time this person entered until the time he left, it was a matter of a few minutes. Taken together, this told me this person had been in the building before and was extremely familiar with the floor. The tape also captured the time, so I knew the theft occurred at 7:25 A.M.

The next day, at about 6:30 A.M., my security manager and I went back to the building and stood in the lobby. No guarantee but I felt this was an experienced burglar who considered this office easy pickings. Low and behold at about 7:10 A.M., we had a person entering the lobby with a hoodie under a short leather jacket, with the letters GAP prominently displayed in the front. As he proceeded further in the lobby, I walked toward him. As we made eye contact, he asked me whether there was a coffee machine in the building. At the same time, he motioned with his hand, as if he was attempting to drink coffee. As I continued toward him, I said I wasn't sure and I wanted to talk to him. This exchange took place in seconds. As I got closer, he made a u-turn and ran out of the building. I took off after him.

I went from 45th and Madison Avenue down to Grand Central Station, where I lost him. It wasn't until I got back to the building that I realized I had shed my coat in the lobby when I took off after him. I knew that the MTA police had an office in the area, and my hope was that an officer would quickly recognize there was a "hot pursuit" and assist me in the arrest. Although the suspect got away, not all was lost. I made arrangements to look at a photo spread of potential suspects at Midtown South. After reviewing over a hundred photographs, I was able to identify our guy. He had been arrested several times for burglaries at midtown Manhattan office buildings, and his last known address was a homeless shelter. Although I had retired, those DEA investigative skills had not left me.

The police asked me to get our employee to file a report as the complainant. I had everything lined up so he would not have to go to the precinct; he could give a statement over the phone. My elation at making progress in this investigation was tempered when I found out our complainant had ignored my calls, took a day off, and did not want to file a complaint. Later on, at a meeting of private security executives, my peers informed me once this guy was off our property, they probably would not have chased him. In effect, he was no longer a problem and the end game in corporate security is not always arrest and prosecution. I've always given 100 percent so it was hard to face reality that I could have been injured chasing a thief who had stolen a laptop and the victim could care less. Ron's advice kicked in again: "Protect Lew Rice."

September 11, 2001, is the day that changed the role of corporate security in America forever. One of the benefits of being in the private sector is that I get to network with the other security directors, people I knew when we were all on the front line in law enforcement.

On September 10, Bob Littlejohn (formerly Avon), Charles Steadman (KPMG), Scott Nelson (formerly AOL Time Warner), and I spent the night at Pete O'Neill's house. We were going fishing the next day for striped bass at Montauk Point. Pete, as usual, was the ultimate host. He barbecued that night and the next day at about 4 A.M., we headed to Montauk Point. Scott Nelson, my boss at the time, returned to the city. There's an empowering feeling of exhilaration sitting in that chair, bringing that twenty-five pound striped bass in. During the course of the morning, the captain told us there were reports of a plane crashing into the Twin Towers. We all considered this another one of many "that's life in the city" stories. When we got back to the dock at around 11 A.M., we saw the true extent of the devastation on CNN—both towers imploding. Pete, realizing the gravity of the situation, extended the invitation to stay at his house until things settled down. However, the sense of mission kicked in, so Bob and I immediately headed back to the city. I told Bob first, I had my retired DEA credentials and second, you're white, I'm black. The police will assume we're cops and wave us on. They did and we made it back to the city in record time. At intervals on the LIE, as we approached a road block, I displayed the badge in the window and we continued on non-stop. When we arrived in the city, we were struck by the faces of New Yorkers. Those who were still in the city had that blank stare, one of desperation and confusion. These devastating attacks had shaken this city.

In the months that followed, the President created the Department of Homeland Security by merging over twenty federal agencies into one. This was the largest reorganization of the federal government since World War II. Homeland Security, unlike National Security, is a shared responsibility between the government and the private sector. This is critically important since 85 percent of the country's infrastructure is owned by the private sector. In this arrangement, the private sector has the opportunity to get the edge. In life, information is power. If you hire the "right" security person, he/she should be well respected within the industry, be able to access the government network, and bring back the necessary information from which the company can make critical decisions. I can recall quite vividly the remarks of the leader of an intelligence agency when he spoke to a group of private security executives. His words and demeanor indicated he was extremely comfortable with the group since he had worked with many of us in the room and was also quite familiar with our former organizations. Six years after the creation of the Department of Homeland Security, we still find this new agency trying to establish itself with the law enforcement/security network. When concerns arise regarding the safety of Corporate America, who should be the voice of the dissemination of information? Should it be the FBI, CIA, or the Department of Homeland Security? This is extremely important because when there is a crisis in the nation, the public needs to be able to quickly identify the leader and the organization that will deliver us to peace and tranquility. The new focus on corporate security brought about the elevation in duties, respect, and responsibility for the Chief Security Officer. Several of my peers received a promotion or were recruited to other companies based on their experience and background. 9-11 forced Corporate America to reevaluate the security position and ensure they had a highly skilled seasoned executive in this portion. The relationship between Homeland Security and the private sector continues to evolve with each side adjusting and attempting to provide value to the other.

One of the best parts of my job is the ability to stay connected to my former associates in law enforcement. As one travels around the world, you realize how fortunate we are to have dedicated men and women protecting our country and way of life.

More Undercover

THE NEXT TWO CASES WERE STARTED BY MY FORMER PARTNER, BILL, ONE of the best undercover agents, who plied his trade on the streets of New York. The scene is the late 1970s prior to the office ban on working cocaine investigations. It was the Labor Day weekend, and Bill was on vacation. One of his sources, who was facing fifteen years to life on state charges, called Frank and said that the subject to whom he had previously introduced Bill was ready to deal. As I picked up my phone that Sunday afternoon—these were the days before caller ID—and heard Frank's voice, I knew my holiday plans were over. The end of summer barbeque with family and friends would have to wait.

After exchanging pleasantries, I met Frank and two other team members, John and George, at the office in midtown. It seemed most of our group was out of town; however, Frank, never one to turn down the chance to arrest a drug dealer, was ready to go. What we lost in numbers we made up in spirit and experience. The plan was for me to join our confidential source (CS) in his house on the East Side of Manhattan and await the drug dealer who would deliver to me a couple of ounces of cocaine. Although our target had already met with Bill, I was substituted as Bill's cousin, who was ready to do the deal while Bill was out of town.

At about eight o'clock, Simon came to the CS's apartment and after greetings were exchanged, we got down to business. We immediately developed a bond, and I learned although his father had died, he was still ready to complete the deal. I must admit I was not encouraging him to continue on. This being the last holiday weekend of the summer, I could tell my teammates would not have been disappointed if this deal was postponed and they could continue with their end-of-summer plans.

Those unfortunate souls who answered their phones were now stuck. We had no idea when this investigation would end. He also said his house was filled with people but I should follow him home to Brooklyn and he would get the four ounces of cocaine. Narcotics work is never nine-to-five, weekends off. Reality had set in; we had a legitimate drug dealer who was ready to sell me felony weight cocaine. By now, you know the rest—off we went to Brooklyn. I left the source in his apartment, left the lobby, said goodbye to the doorman and followed him to Brooklyn.

About forty minutes later, when we got to Flatbush Avenue near the Belt Parkway, he pulled over and asked me to wait for him to return. He returned a short time later, entered my car, and gave me four ounces of cocaine. As I examined the cocaine, I put on the emergency lights, our pre-arranged bust signal. At the same time, I got out of the car to retrieve the money from my jacket in the back seat. As soon as I opened the door, I heard those famous words: "Freeze mother f...! You're under arrest!" I must admit, Simon looked dazed and confused; however, he quickly regained his composure when Frank told him that although we were federal agents this was a state case and he was facing fifteen years to life for a drug sale to a federal undercover agent.

His metamorphosis was quick. He said he had his source's telephone number back in the house and was willing to call him and set him up to be arrested. As we uncuffed him, Frank told him he had exactly six minutes to return and if he was not back in six minutes, the four of us would be in his house, turning it upside down, looking for him, and it would be obvious to his mother, close family, and friends that he was a drug dealer. Needless to say, Simon was back within four and a half minutes with the telephone number.

Now to phase two: We told him to call his source and confirm that he had sold the four ounces of cocaine and had his money. We also told him to tell his source that we were satisfied with the coke and were ready to purchase more, right now, if he had it. At the conclusion of the call, Simon told us the source, Freddy, had an ounce of heroin available for sale. We told Simon to call him back, get the price for the ounce, and tell him we wanted it. Since Frank was familiar with the area, he selected a diner on Flatbush Avenue as our meeting spot. Simon called Freddy again and told him to bring the heroin to the diner in about twenty minutes.

Our plan now was that after Freddy gave me the heroin, I would go to the bathroom, look it over, and come out with my leather jacket in my hand. This was the visual signal that he had given me the heroin and the arrest could be made. I took a seat in a booth facing the door and a short time later, I saw a man enter who fit the description of Freddy. I had told Freddy to give me his description, including what he was wearing. Seated a few stools in front of me was John, another agent on our team. After greetings were exchanged, Freddy gave me the heroin under the table. I excused myself and went to the bathroom. I entered the stall and examined the ounce of heroin. Satisfied that I had the goods, I left the bathroom with my leather jacket on my arm. John's eyes were on me, I smiled and sat back down. In one motion, John left his stool and put his gun to Freddy's head and with his other hand, he placed his badge before Freddy's eyes. I could see the fear and anxiety in his face. On one hand, he was happy he wasn't dead but on the other hand, he knew he was going to jail for a long time.

We made the same pitch to Freddy. Where did you get the coke and heroin? Freddy didn't hesitate: He said his source was Walter and he was staying in the Hilton Hotel. He was supposed to call him once the deal went down. We now had two prisoners in tow and we, the four agents, were off to the Hilton Hotel in midtown. Once we got there, we determined Walter's room and had Freddy call from the lobby and say he would be right up. A few minutes later, Freddy knocked on the door and Walter opened up. We stormed in with our guns. "Freeze, Walter! You're under arrest!" In plain view, we saw hundreds of pills and several thousand dollars. There was also an eighteen- year old girl in a nightgown. We found out later she was Walter's daughter-in-law. Yes, Walter's son was away in the army and Walter was with his son's wife in a hotel room in New York City. Walter was about sixty years old—obviously a lifelong degenerate criminal. He quickly assessed the situation and asked to speak with Frank alone. Frank said, "Okay, let's talk," and told me to come with him. We went into the bathroom—me, Frank, and Walter—and as we closed the door, Walter said, "I used to work for you guys on the West Coast, so I know how you guys work. If you let the girl go and let me keep the money, I can do some good things for you." Frank didn't miss a beat. He responded, "I don't know what kind of a deal you had out West, but this is 1977. You go, the girl goes, and also the money and pills." What a night. Marian's words are coming back: "Drug dealers are the scum of the earth."

The next case where I had a significant role was the Freddy Ramos investigation. During the late seventies, Bill was one of the few agents who had penetrated the hierarchy of the Colombian cocaine network and was buying pounds and kilos of cocaine. The Freddy Ramos investigation was a major coup for the group. Bill was purchasing pounds of high-quality cocaine from a cagey South American dealer. Sterling Johnson, currently a U.S. District Court Judge, Eastern District of New York, was the Special Narcotics Prosecutor then and had provided us with the buy money for this case; consequently, the prosecution and any informants derived from the investigation would be given to his office.

On the day in question, Bill had made arrangements to buy a kilogram of cocaine from "Freddy." There had been several meetings between Bill and Freddy, which led to this day. We were to meet in Brooklyn at Freddy's house at 6 A.M. Although Freddy never told Bill where he lived, we were able to determine his residence after an exhaustive background investigation. Since I was a junior agent and I didn't have a car, I was to ride with a senior agent, Jim, who lived in Queens. He was to pick me up at 5 A.M. and then we would meet Frank and the rest of the group at Freddy's house. The goal was to follow him from his house to his meeting with Bill in midtown. At about 5:10 A.M., when I didn't hear from Jim, I tried to reach him on my portable radio—no answer. Forty-five minutes later, I was still waiting and quite concerned. This was a major operation, and we were a tight group that prided ourselves on teamwork. I really didn't think anything was wrong with Jim. He had a history of disciplinary problems during his short time in New York. He was a nice guy but extremely immature. He was an agent in his early thirties, but the only thing he could teach me was what not to do. He was famous for calling in and requesting a day off because his mother died, his father died, his grandmother died—you get the picture. In fact, one of the supervisors said if half of the deaths in his family were true, he's had more tragedy in his life than the Kennedy family.

At about 7:30 A.M., Jim arrived and we headed out to Brooklyn. I can't remember the excuse he gave for being late. I was more concerned about my reputation. I didn't want to be considered unreliable, and I also didn't want to miss out on the action. Narcotics work requires honesty, dependability, and resourcefulness: the ultimate qualities for winning teams.

When we arrived at Freddy's house, the surveillance had moved to Manhattan. Freddy had left that morning, and the group followed him. This is a crucial point in the surveillance: We needed to document all of our target's movements before he delivered the drugs to the undercover agent. We may be able to identify his sources or the location where he picked up the cocaine. We were a couple of hours late. Frank was probably not happy, so he told us to stand by in Brooklyn, stay at the house. Up until this time, I had a good reputation. I was determined not to jeopardize it. If I had to work with Jim again, I would request a reassignment.

The next couple of hours were spent in silence. At about 10 A.M., we saw Freddy's wife, Karen, leave the house and enter the car. We notified Frank and the team via the portable radio and followed her into Manhattan. The excitement increased as we entered midtown following Karen in the car and we heard the broadcast transmission of the team in the city following Freddy on foot. The surveillance team observed Freddy enter Bloomingdale's as we followed Karen to a parking lot, where she parked and began to walk toward the Third Avenue entrance of Bloomingdale's. I got out of the car and followed her. She entered the revolving door, with me right behind her.

Karen positioned herself inside Bloomingdale's near the revolving door. As I walked into the store, I noticed the hand-off. Seconds later, Freddy walked through the revolving door, and with the grace and speed of a NFL quarterback, Karen handed him a package as Freddy entered the inside of the store. He continued through the revolving door out into the street and delivered a kilogram of coke to Bill. I must say, I was impressed with their timing and choreography. That maneuver, however, brought Karen fifteen years in the state prison.

Nicky Barnes was one of the country's top heroin dealers. I'm probably one of the few agents or police officers who will admit he had nothing to do with this major case. However, a few of us would sit in the back of the courtroom during his trial, hiding our faces since we were working undercover. For us new agents, it was like getting a Ph.D. in narcotic enforcement. In 2007, the thirtieth anniversary of his conviction, he wrote a book and will star in a movie based on his life.

Although I'm retired, some investigations and challenges still fascinate me. Nicky talks about the arrest of Matty Madonna in his book. Madonna was his heroin supplier throughout the seventies. I was involved in Madonna's arrest back then, but I had no idea he was Nicky's supplier. The scene for the arrest was the summer of 1977 or '78. We had just come back to the office from a deal that did not end up with a drug buy or arrest. It was a Friday night and although it was nine o'clock, the evening was not wasted. It was still early enough to enjoy the nightlife in the city.

Suddenly the phone rang, it was agents from the Hawaii office. We were the response group for this part of the world, responsible for providing administrative and investigative assistance for their cases. They had arrested a New Yorker with four kilograms of heroin. He had decided to cooperate, and the delivery would take place in New York.

Frank's eyes lit up. Four kilos of heroin and arrests in New York. As we worked through the details, the agents would arrive at JFK with the defendant the following day in the afternoon. The group was figuring we'd go home, come back Saturday, and set up the surveillance at JFK and the other identified locations in the city. By now you know Frank had other ideas. We all headed up to the Bronx, to the confidential source's (CS) apartment. That's right—it's nine o'clock on Friday night and the agents will not arrive at JFK until the afternoon the following day.

Bill and I had a yellow Cadillac, which the tech agent wired for audio. This vehicle would be used by the CS if he could get the heroin recipient into the car to record the conversation. We spent the night in the cars. At about three in the morning, two uniform NYPD officers on patrol shined the light in our car. Can you imagine the visual: two black guys, one in the front and one in the back, sleeping in a yellow caddy in the Bronx? After we woke up, we flashed our badges and went back to sleep. At the first shot of dawn, fifteen guys, one by one, entered the CS's apartment. We took cold showers, put on the same clothes, and got back in our cars. That afternoon we arrested Madonna for possession with intent to distribute heroin. Thirty years later, I read Nicky's book and found out he was Nicky's source. So I guess I did have something to do with the Barnes' case: We arrested his source.

As I reflect on my career with the DEA, I must say I had a great run. I got to travel the world and work with some of this country's heroes. People ask me constantly if I miss it. Yes, I do, but nobody can take your memories. For twenty-six years and three months, no matter what the challenge, problems, or controversy, I woke up every day, went to work, and got a good feeling from helping people for no other reason other than it was the right thing to do.